220

220 Projects for Cascade 220

Editor: Dara Tatum
Art Direction: Patti Pierce Stone
Technical Editing: Julie Meyers

Contributing Designers:
Mary Lou Egan
Urban Tribal Wear Designs
Elizabeth Wellenstein
Patti Pierce Stone
Mary McSweeny

Model Knitters:
Mary Knapp   Lynn Dunaway
Karen Harris   JoAnn Varda
Ellen Schneider   Mary McSweeny

Montat
Publishing

220 - 220 Projects for Cascade 220
© 2005, Montat Publishing
All rights reserved.
ISBN #0-0729007-9-9

www.montat.com
www.the220book.com
Printed in the United States of America

Why is Cascade 220 different from other wools?

Cascade 220 is spun exclusively from Peruvian Highland Wool. This wool is the result of a serendipitous cross breeding between the pure bred Merino Sheep and the local sheep belonging to the indigenous highland herders.

A few land holders in Peru held most of the Merino sheep in the country and this chance breeding occurred during one of Peru's land reforms, when in an effort to provide a means of livelihood to the impoverished native population these merino sheep were distributed to the indigenous population. These native sheepherders often kept them with their existing stock and, sheep being sheep, they ignored the difference between the two breeds and proceeded to cross breed.

This cross breeding of the native stock and the purebred European stock produced unique and wonderful wool which we call Highland Wool. This wool is very white, thus it can be dyed in light colors without bleaching. Like the wool from the native sheep Highland Wool has a lot of crimp, giving it that extra loft for softness and warmth. Equally, Peruvian Highland Wool has a very long staple, so it resists pilling. To make a long story short, this chance breeding has produced a wool that is perfect for hand knitting.

We are thrilled that Montat Publishing has selected Cascade 220 for their book and hope that you enjoy working with what we feel is a very special wool.

CASCADE YARNS
DISTRIBUTOR OF FINE YARN

from the editor. . .

A variation on a theme - that was my original idea when I began this project. I had already selected the yarn. Cascade 220 provided me with a wonderful and versitile wool, available in a vast array of colors. I wanted a collection of patterns with variations on each that would give the knitter a choice of colors, textures, finsihing, and techniques. The variations could also offer ideas for use in other projects - fabulous color combinations, unique stitch patterns, interchanging to create endless possibilities.

The projects included in this collection are traditional, trendy, and some are downright funky. I think there is something for every knitter, of every experience level. I hope that you agree, and that you do not limit yourself to the colorways shown, or the particular texture patterns given. Explore and experiment with your own favorite colors, or add a different stitch motif to the patterns offered.

I gathered a group of talented designers to assist me with my goal. I cannot thank them enough for their effort, creativity, and contributions to this book. So, to Mary Lou Egan, Elizabeth Wellenstein, Patti Pierce Stone, Mary McSweeny, and the Urban Tribal Wear Design Team, I simply say that this book would not have been completed without your talent and dedication.

Special thanks goes out to the folks at Cascade Yarn, for their support, and for such great yarn!

Dara

Capelets
design by Urban Tribal Wear Designs

Finished Size
S(M)

Gauge
5.5 sts x 7 rows = 1"

Seed Stitch
Row 1: *k1, p1; rep from *, end k1
Rep row 1

Materials
1 skein # 9408 (Cordovan, Color 1)
1 skein #9338 (Lichen, Color 2)
1 skein #2438 (Spring Meadow, Color 3)
1 skein #4011 (Sparrow, Color 4)
1 skein #8415 (Cranberry, Color 5)

US 7 (4.5 mm) ndl
US 6 (4.0 mm) ndl

Directions
With larger ndl and Color 1, CO 54 sts and work foundation row (row 1 of Chart 1) as follows: k1, pm, k1(seam stitch), pm, k10, pm, k1 (seam stitch), pm, k28, pm, k1 (seam stitch), pm, k10, pm, k1(seam stitch), pm, k1. Work chart, continuing at row 2. Purl 1 row.

Begin increases
Inc 8 sts every RS row 3 times as follows: *k to marker, yo, slip marker, k1, slip marker, yo, repeat from * to the end of the row (78 sts). Then inc 10 sts every RS row as follows until there are 16 sts before the first marker, ending with a WS row: k1, m1, *k to marker, yo, slip marker, k1, slip marker, yo, repeat from * to one st before the end of the row, m1, k last st (137 sts). Then work the following increase pattern 14 times:

Row 1: *k to marker, yo, slip marker, k1, slip marker, yo, repeat from *
Row 2: purl
Row 3: *k to 2 sts before the next marker, k2tog, yo, slip marker, k1, slip marker, yo, k2tog, repeat from *
Row 4: purl

Work 4 rows even. To shape bottom edge, dec once at each edge every RS row 4 times. Work WS row. Bind off 2 sts at beg of next 2 rows, then bind off 3 sts at beg of next 2 rows. Bind off 5 sts at beg of next 2 rows. Leave sts on ndl.

Pattern 1

Finishing edge
With Color 3 and smaller ndl, with RS facing, pick up 50 sts starting at upper left edge, work across sts on ndl, pick up 50 sts at the right edge. Work in seed st for 1½". Bind off in pattern.

Collar
With Color 5 and smaller ndl, with RS facing, pick up 24 neck edge sts, 11 sleeve sts, 28 back neck sts, 11 sleeve sts, and 24 neck edge sts. Work back and forth in k2, p2 rib for 4". Bind off loosely in rib.

Embroidery
Using a piece of contrasting scrap yarn, lay out a squiggle design over rows 14-26 (Color 3). When happy with the design, pin it in place and embroider stem stitch alongside the scrap yarn with Color 5. Embroider French knots as desired to highlight the design. Then work a cross stitch pattern with Color 5 as shown on pattern rows 50 and 51.

Flower
With Color 5 and smaller ndl, CO 50 sts. Work 4 rows in st st. On the next RS row *k1, m1, repeat from * to the end of the row. Work 3 rows in st st. Bind off. Roll the strip into a rose and stitch the layers in place along the bottom. Sew a 1½" pin onto the bottom of the flower.

Leaf
With Color 2 and smaller ndl, CO 4 sts.
Row 1: (RS): knit
Row 2 and all even rows: purl
Row 3: k2, m1, k2
Row 5: k2, m1, k1, m1, k2
Row 7: k3, m1, k1, m1, k3
Row 9: k4, m1, k1, m1, k4
Row 11: k5, m1, k1, m1, k5
Row 13/15/17: knit
Bind off. Gather bottom of leaf and stitch to the bottom of the rose.

Variation: Hooded Capelet
Directions
Work capelet as described in the main pattern up to collar section. Work hood as follows: With Color 5 and larger ndl, with RS facing, pick up 26 right front neck sts, 14 back neck sts, pm, pick up rem 14 back neck sts, pick up 27 front left sts (71 sts). Turn. Work 1 row. On next row (RS), establish a seed st border over the first and last 6 sts, work st st between border sts. Work as established for 3".
Increase 1 st on each side of center back marker every right side row 7 times, then every 3 rows 20 times. Bind off when the piece measures 13½". Sew the top seam.

Variation: Capelet with Shawl Collar
Directions
Work capelet as described in the main pattern up to collar section. Work a 5" shawl collar as follows: with Color 5 and smaller ndl, with RS facing, begin at right neck edge and pick up 76 sts evenly around the neck. Turn. With RS facing, work the first 19 sts in seed st, pm, work 38 sts in seed st, pm, turn. Shape collar with short rows as follows:
*work back to opposite shawl marker, remove marker, wrap next st, turn. Repeat from * until all sts are worked. Work even for 1". Bind off loosely in pattern.

Variation: Two-color Capelet
Materials
4 skeins main color
2 skeins contrast color

Directions
Work capelet in st st as described in the main pattern, using main color. Use contrast color for the edging and collar of choice.

Variation: Capelet with Lacing Closure
Directions
Work capelet as described in the main pattern and any variation, replacing the finishing edge with the lacing closure.

Lacing closure
With Color 3 and smaller ndl, with RS facing, pick up 50 sts starting at the upper left edge, work across sts on ndl, pick up 50 sts on right edge. Work in seed st for 2 rows. In the next row, work eyelets (k4, yo, 2tog) 4 times, continue in seed st to opposite side, work 4 more eyelets. Continue in seed st until the edge measures 1½". Bind off loosely in seed st. Make a 36" length of 3-st I-cord in contrast color. Lace through the eyelets and tie in a loose bow. Ribbon can also be used.

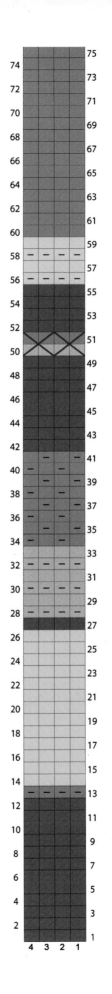

Chart 1

☐ knit
— purl

Dome Hats
design by Elizabeth Wellenstein

Lingonberry Hat
Finished Sizes
S (M, L) 18 (20, 22)"

Materials
1 skein #2410 (Purple; MC)
½ skein #8407 (Oyster; CC)
½ skein #8885 (Dark Plum; CC)
US 5 (3.75 mm) 16" circ ndl, or size to obtain gauge
Set of US 5 dpn, or size to match larger ndls
US 3 (3.25 mm) 16" circ ndl
Gauge
6 sts x 7 rows = 1" worked with larger ndls in the round with 2 colors

Directions
Body
With smaller ndl, CO 108 (120, 132) sts. Pm and join ends, being careful not to twist the circle. Knit 6 rnds.
Rnd 7: *k2tog, yo, rep from * to end of rnd. Change to larger ndls. Knit 5 rnds. At this point either keep knitting and whipstitch the hem in place once the hat is complete, or knit the hem to the hat as follows: fold the fabric at the K2tog/yo row, which creates a picot edge. With a dpn, pick up each st along the cast-on edge (one at a time) and knit together with the corresponding live st on your

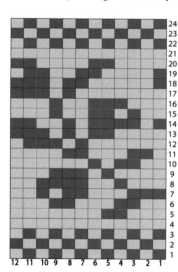

Chart A

circular ndl. Continue around entire row. Work rows 1-24 of Chart A.
Crown
In the next rnd, using MC, inc or dec evenly as follows: inc 4 to 112 sts (dec 1

Pattern 6

to 119, inc 1 to 133). Work rows 1-32 of Chart B beginning at row 7 (5, 1). When the sts no longer fit comfortably around the ndl, switch to dpns. At the end of Chart B, 7 sts remain.

Finishing
Continue k2tog until 4 sts remain. Knit I-cord for 2" as follows: k4 onto one dpn. Slide sts to opposite end of ndl and transfer it to your left hand. Repeat. Break yarn, leaving 6" for a finishing strand. With yarn ndl and strand, join the 4 I-cord loops together and pull the strand down through the center of the cord. Tack down at the base on the inside

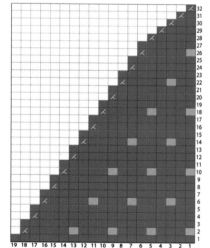

Chart B

丿 k2tog

of the hat. Tie a knot at the base of the I-cord. Weave in ends.

Variation: Carousel Hat
Finished Sizes
S (M, L) 17½ (20, 23)"
Materials
1 skein #8234 (Pistachio)

Gauge
5.5 sts x 9 rows = 1" worked in the round in seed st (Rows 1-2 of Chart C).

Directions
Body
CO 96 (112, 128) sts. Pm and join ends, being careful not to twist the circle. Knit 15 rnds. Work rows 1-33 of Chart C. To make bobble: [K1, P1] 2 times in same st, turn, p4, turn, sl 2, k2tog, p2sso.

Crown
In the next rnd, inc or dec evenly as follows: inc 2 to 98 sts, (inc 0 to 112, dec 2 to 126). Work rows 1-32 of Chart B for crown beginning at row 11 (7, 3). When the sts no longer fit comfortably around the ndl, switch to dpns. At the end of Chart B, 7 sts remain. Finish as described for main pattern.

Variation: Checks and Bobbles
Finished Sizes
S (M, L) 18 (20, 22)"

Materials
1 skein #8010 (Natural)

Gauge
5.5 sts x 9 rows = 1" worked in the round in seed st (Rows 3 and 4 of Chart D)

Directions
Body
With smaller circ ndl, CO 100 (110, 120) sts. Pm and join ends, being careful not to twist the circle. Knit 6 rnds.

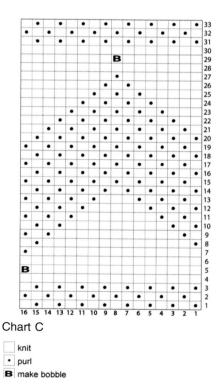

Chart C

☐ knit
• purl
B make bobble

Pattern 7

Rnd 7: *k2tog, yo, rep from * to end of rnd. Change to larger ndls. Knit 5 rnds. At this point either keep knitting and whipstitch the hem in place once the hat is complete, or knit the hem to the hat as described in main pattern. Work rows 1-32 of Chart D.

Crown

Inc or dec evenly in next round as follows: dec 2 to 98 sts (inc 2 to 112, dec 1 to 119). Work rows 1-32 of Chart B for crown beginning at row 11 (7, 5).

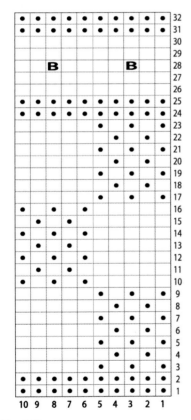

Chart D

When the sts no longer fit comfortably around the ndl, switch to dpns. At the end of Chart B, 7 sts remain. Finish as described for main pattern.

Variation: Flower Dome Hat
Finished Sizes
S (M, L) 16 (19, 21)"
Materials
1 skein #8234 (Pistachio; MC)
½ skein #8010 (Natural; CC)

Gauge
6 sts x 7 rows = 1" knit in the round with 2 colors

Directions
Body
With MC, CO 96 (112, 128) sts. Pm and join ends, being careful not to twist the circle. Knit 15 rounds. Work rows 1-25 of Chart E.

Crown
With MC, inc or dec evenly in next rnd as follows: inc 2 to 98 sts, (inc 0 to 112, dec 2 to 126). Work rows 1-32 of Chart B for the crown beginning at row 11 (7, 3). When the sts no longer fit comfortably around the ndl, switch to dpns. At the end of Chart B, 7 sts remain. Finish as described for main pattern.

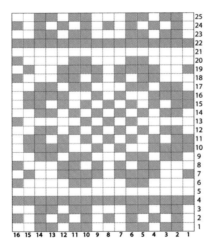

Chart E

Pattern 8

Variation: Mystery Hat
Finished Sizes
S (M, L) 20 (21, 23)"
Materials
1 skein #2410 (Purple; MC)
½ skein #8234 (Pistachio; CC)

Gauge
6 sts x 7 rows = 1" knit in the round with 2 colors

Directions
Body
With MC, CO 120 (128, 136) sts. Pm and join ends, being careful not to twist the circle. Knit 15 rounds. Work rows 1-27 of Chart F.

Crown
With MC, inc or dec evenly in next round as follows: dec 1 to 119 sts, (dec 2 to 126, dec 3 to 133). Work rows 1-32 of Chart B for crown beginning at row 5 (3, 1). When the sts no longer fit comfortably around the ndl, switch to dpns. At the end of Chart B, 7 sts remain. Finish as described for main pattern.

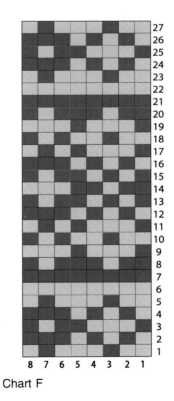

Chart F

Library Shawls
design by Patti Pierce Stone

Finished size
Approx 18" x 70"

Materials
5 skeins, #4011 (Sparrow)
US 7 (4.5mm) 24" circ ndl
Set of US 7 (4.5mm) dpn

Gauge
19 st x 25 rows = 4" worked in st st

Faux Cable Rib
Row 1: (WS): k2, *p2, yo, rep from * to last 2 sts; end sl 2 wyif (127 sts)
Row 2: k5, p3so, *k3, p3so, rep from * to last 2 sts; sl 2 wyif (86 sts)

Right Faux Cable
Note: The right edge may have a tendency to draw up a bit. To compensate, wrap twice when knitting the first st on the RS rows. Drop the second wrap on the return row.
Row 1: (and all WS rows): [p2, yo] twice, k1, p8, k1, [p2, yo] twice, sl 2 wyif
Row 2: k2, [k3, p3so) twice, p1, yo, k3, ssk, k3, p1, [k3, p3so] twice
Row 4: k2, [k3, p3so] twice, p1, k1, yo, k3, ssk, k2, p1, [k3, p3so] twice
Row 6: k2, [k3, p3so] twice, p1, k2, yo, k3, ssk, k1, p1, [k3, p3so] twice
Row 8: k2, [k3, p3so] twice, p1, k3, yo, k3, ssk, p1, [k3, p3so] twice

Left Faux Cable
Row 1: (and all WS rows): k2, [p2, yo] twice, k1, p8, k1, [p2, yo] twice
Row 2: [k3, p3so] twice, p1, k3, k2tog, k3, yo, p1, [k3, p3so] twice, sl 2 wyif
Row 4: [k3, p3so] twice, p1, k2, k2tog, k3, yo, k1, p1, [k3, p3so] twice, sl 2 wyif
Row 6: [k3, p3so] twice, p1, k1, k2tog, k3, yo, k2, p1, [k3, p3so] twice, sl 2 wyi
Row 8: [k3, p3so] twice, p1, k2tog, k3, yo, k3, p1, [k3, p3so] twice, sl 2 wyif

Directions
Main section
CO 86 sts using a provisional cast-on method. K2, p2 to the last 2 sts, sl 2 wyif. Work Faux Cable Rib four times. On last row, pm between sts 20/21 and between 66/67. Work main section as follows: On RS rows, work Right Faux Cable, knit sts between markers, work Left Faux Cable. On WS rows, work Left Faux Cable pattern, purl sts between markers, work Right Faux Cable. Work rows 1 – 8 of both patterns once, then rows 1 – 7.
Note: st count is different between WS rows (94 sts) and RS rows (86 sts).

Pattern 11

Work pocket section
Work pocket anchor row (RS) as follows: work Right Faux Cable Row 8, k9, p28, k9, work Left Faux Cable Row 8. Work as in main section for 32 rows (4 pattern rep), replacing the st st between the markers with the following two rows to create the sides of the pocket:
WS rows: p9, k1, p26, k1, p9
RS rows: k9, p1, k26, p1, k9

Continue as in main section, with st st between markers, 40 more times or until wrap is 10 in shorter than desired length. Work a second pocket section, starting with the 32 rows to create sides and ending with the Pocket Anchor row. Work the main section rows twice more, beginning with row 3 of Left/Right Faux Cable patterns. Then work a transition row (RS) as follows: k2, [k3, p3so] twice, k10, [k3, p3so] twice, k to marker, [k3, p3so] twice, k10, [k3, p3so] twice, sl 2 wyif. Work Faux Cable Rib 4 times; on the next row k2, p2 across. Bind off.

Add pockets
With RS facing, place the purl loop of the 28 purl sts of the pocket bottom anchor row onto one of the dpns.
At the beg and end of each pocket row, work the top loop of the purl stitch at the

pocket's edge together with the first/last st. Work 23 pocket rows as follows, ending on WS row:
RS: knit first st with top loop of purl, knit to last st; knit last st with top loop of purl, turn
WS: purl(tbl) first st with top loop of purl, purl to last st; purl last st with top loop of purl, turn

Work 4 rep of Faux Cable Rib, continuing to work the last st tog with the purl st at pocket edge. Add a knit st at the beg and end of the RS rows and a purl stitch on the WS rows. Bind off using a decrease bind-off method, being sure to anchor the last st on both sides. Repeat for second pocket.

Finishing
Remove provisional cast-on and remount stitches. Cast off using a decrease bind-off method so that the two ends match. Weave in all ends and block.

Variation: Basketweave Mesh Shawl
Materials
5 skeins #2414 (Ginger)

Garter Stitch Border
Knit across to last 2 st, sl 2 wyif (86 st)

Right Basketweave
Row 1 (RS): k6, k1, [yo, rt] 4 times, k1, k4
Row 2/4: k4, p2, [p2tog, p1] 4 times, k4, sl 2 wyif
Row 3: k6, lt, [yo, lt] 4 times, k4
Rows 5 – 8: rep rows 1 – 4

Left Basketweave
Row 1 (RS): k4, k1, [yo, rt] 4 times, k1, k4, sl 2 wyif
Row 2/4: k6, p2, [p2tog, p1] 4 times, k4
Row 3: k4, lt, [yo, lt] 4 times, k4, sl 2 wyif
Rows 5 – 8: rep rows 1 – 4

Directions
CO 86 sts using a provisional cast-on method. K2, p2 to the last 2 sts, sl 2 wyif. Work 8 rows of Garter Stitch Border. On last row, pm between stitches 20/21 and between 66/67. Work main section as follows: on RS rows, work Right Basketweave, knit sts between markers, work Left Basketweave; on WS rows, work Left Basketweave, purl sts between markers, work Right Basketweave. Work rows 1 – 8 of both patterns once, then rows 1 – 7. Work pocket anchor row (WS) as follows: work Left Basketweave row 8, p9, k28, p9, work Right Basketweave row 8. Finish as described in the main pattern.

Easy Scarves
design by Montat Designs

Drop Stitch Scarf
Materials
1 skein # 4001 (Bluestone)
1 skein # 8011 (Aspen Heather)
US 8 (5 mm) ndl
Gauge is not important for this project.
Directions
Carry both colors together.
CO 24 sts.
Row 1-4: knit
Row 5: *k1,yo twice; rep from *
Row 6: knit, dropping yo sts as you work across
Continue working rows 1-6 until scarf is desired length, ending at Row 4. Bind off.

Curly Q Boa Scarf
Materials
1 skein, shown in #9433 (Quatro)
US 9 (5.5 mm) ndl
Gauge is not important for this project.
Directions
CO 120 sts.
Row 1 and all odd rows: knit
Row 2 and all even rows: knit into the front and back of each stitch
Row 7: knit
Bind off.

Elizabeth's Scarf
Finished Size
Totally up to you! Your scarf will be several feet long. The more rows you knit, the wider the scarf will be.
Gauge
Your choice: a US 8 needle will make a denser fabric and a US 10 will make a looser fabric.

Materials
Leftover yarn of various colors, about 1 skein (220 yds) total.
US 8 (5.0 mm), size 9 (5.5 mm) or US 10 (6.0 mm) 29" (80 cm) circ ndl

Directions
CO 240 sts with size 8, 220 sts with size 9, or 200 sts with size 10 ndl. Trim tail yarn to about 5". Cut the ball yarn to about a 5" length and tie it to the next color, about 5". Knit 1 row. Cut yarn, leaving 5", choose next color and tie knot, leaving 5" hanging. Knit 1 row. Continue in this way until the scarf is as wide as you like. The more rows you knit, the wider your scarf will be. Bind off and trim the fringe if necessary to even up the ends.

Pattern 13

Pattern 14

Pattern 15

Skirts
design by Urban Tribal Wear Designs

Finished size
Size XS (S, M, L, XL)
Waist 26 (28, 30, 33, 35)"
Hip 36 (38, 40, 43, 45)"

Materials
6 skeins, shown in # 4011 (Sparrow)
US 7 (4.5 mm) 24" (60 cm) circ ndl
Elastic for waistband, ½" wide

Gauge
5.5 sts x 7 rows = 1"

Directions
CO 144 (156, 164, 184, 192) sts. Pm and join ends, being careful not to twist the circle. Knit 1½". Purl 1 rnd, then knit 2" (this creates the finished edge at the top for the elastic). Knit 72 (78, 82, 92, 96) sts, Pm for center of rnd, knit to end.

Begin shaping for hip
*Knit to within 1 st of marker, m1, k1, slip marker, k1, m1, repeat from * to end of rnd. Increase 4 sts each rnd in this manner every 3 (3, 3, 4, 4) rounds 13 (12, 13, 12, 13) more times (200, 208, 220, 236, 248 sts). Beg at Row 9, work Chart 1 for 16 (17, 18, 19, 20)". Bind off loosely in pattern

Pattern 16

Chart 1

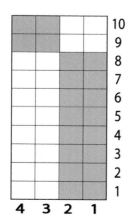

knit
purl

Fold the top down at the purl row and sew waist band with slip stitches, leaving a small opening. Cut a 23 (25, 27, 30, 32)" piece of elastic and thread through the waist band. Overlap the ends of the elastic for 1" and stitch together. Try the skirt on and adjust elastic if needed. Finish sewing waist band.

Variation: Fair Isle Skirt
Materials
1 skein # 4147B (Lemon Yellow; Color 1)
1 skein #7826 (California Poppy; Color 2)
1 skein # 7802 (Cerise; Color 3)
1 skein #7809 (Violet; Color 4)
2 skeins #8902 (Herb; Color 5)

Seed Stitch (worked in the round)
Rnd 1: *k1, p1; rep from *
Rnd 2: *p1, k1; rep from *

Directions
With Color 5, CO and work through hip shaping as described in the main pattern. Work Chart 2 until color pattern section measures 16 (17, 18, 19, 20)". With Color 4, dec 1 st, then work 5 rnds in seed stitch. Bind off loosely in seed stitch. Finish as described in the main pattern.

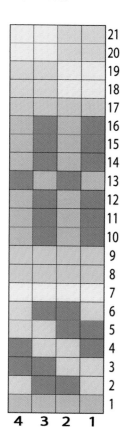

Chart 2

Variation: Three-Color Skirt
Materials
2 skeins #9408 (Cordovan; Color 1)
2 skeins #9429 (Mossy Rock; Color 2)
2 skeins #4001 (Bluestone; Color 3)

Directions
With Color 1, CO and work through hip shaping as described in the main pattern. Work Chart 3 until the color pattern section measures 16 (17, 18, 19, 20)".
Using Color 3, work 5 rnds in garter st (knit 1 rnd, purl 1 rnd). Work points as follows:
K4, turn
K4, turn
K2tog, k2, turn
K3 turn
K3 turn
K2tog, k1, turn
K2 tog turn
Make bobble in last stitch.

Using tapestry needle sew the end of the bobble to the beginning of the bobble making a loop. Weave in loose ends. Join yarn and repeat until all sts have been bound off.

Chart 3

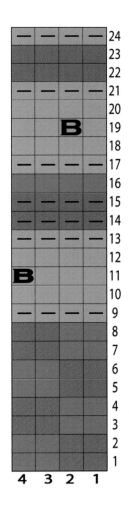

knit
– purl
B make bobble
knit in the front, back and front of the same stitch. Turn. P3, turn, k3, turn, p3, turn, sl 1, k2tog, psso, continue across row as directed.

Variation: Lacy Skirt
Materials
6 skeins, #9345 (Wisteria)

Drop stitch lace pattern
Rnd 1: *p1, k2, p1, rep from * to end of rnd
Rnd 2: *p1, k1, m1, k1, p1, rep from * to end of rnd
Rnd 3-6: *p1, k3, p1, rep from * to end of rnd
Rnd 7: *p1, k1, drop stitch and allow to unravel, k1, p1, rep from * to end of rnd
Rnd 8: rep rnd 1
Rnd 9: *m1, p1, k2, p1, rep from * to end of rnd
Rnd 10-13: *P2, k2, p1, rep from * to end of rnd
Rnd 14: *drop stitch and allow to unravel, p1, k2, p1, rep from * to end of rnd
Rnd 15: rep rnd 1

Directions
CO and work through hip shaping as described in the main pattern. Work Drop Stitch Lace until pattern section measures 16 (17, 18, 19, 20)". Work 5 rnds of rnd 1 of Drop Stitch Lace. Bind off loosely in pattern. Finish as described in the main pattern.

Variation: Skirt with Ruffled Hem
Materials
6 skeins

Seed Stitch (worked in the round)
Rnd 1: *k1, p1; rep from *
Rnd 2: *p1, k1; rep from *

Directions
Work skirt as described in the main pattern. Dec 1 st at end of hip shaping (199, 207, 219, 235, 247 sts). Add ruffle pattern at hem. Work 6 rows of seed st. Bind off in seed st

Ruffle
Rnd 1-3: knit
Rnd 4: *k1, m1, rep from *
Rnd 5-7: knit
Rnd 8: *k2, m1, rep from *
Rnd 9-11: knit

Classic Cardigans
design by Patti Pierce Stone

Finished chest sizes
S (M, L) 36 (38, 40.5)"

Materials
5 (5, 6) skeins, #9435 (Quattro)
US 5 (3.75 mm) 29 or 36" circ ndl
US 7 (4.5mm) 29 or 36" circ ndl
US 7 (4.5 mm) straight ndl
Six ¾" buttons

Gauge
19 st x 24 rows = 4" worked in st st

Directions
CO 154 (160, 168) sts with larger ndl. Do not join the round; this cardigan will be worked flat. Knit across. In next row, increase evenly as follows: K 22 (20, 21), [m1, k 22 (17, 18)] 5 (7, 7) times, m1, k22 (21, 21) for a total of 160 (168, 176 sts). Continue in st st until piece measures 11½ (12, 12½)" and 70 (72, 75 rows) or to 2½" below desired length to armhole.

Right armhole and neck edge shaping
Beginning at the right edge with front cardigan RS facing, k2, ssk, k32 (34, 36). Place rem 124 (130, 136) sts onto a stitch holder or waste yarn to be worked later. Turn and purl back. Work decrease row (RS): k2, ssk, k to end of row; then work 3 rows in st st. Rep these 4 rows 10 (12, 12) times until 24 (24, 26) st remain and 46 (50, 54) rows worked from armhole. Work even for 4 (4, 2) rows or until piece measures 8¼ (9, 9¼)" from armhole. If your row number is different than the stated number, record your row number. Place sts on a stitch holder. Cut yarn, leaving a 24" strand for finishing.

Back
Beginning at the right edge, with RS facing, place 8 (8, 8) sts on a new stitch holder and transfer the next 72 (76, 80) sts to ndl. Leave the rem 44 (46, 48) sts on the stitch holder for left front of sweater and armhole. Work in st st for 50 (54, 56) rows or the number of rows worked for the right front. Place rem back sts on a stitch holder.

Left armhole and neck edge shaping
Beginning at left armhole edge, with RS facing, leave the first 8 (8, 8) sts on the stitch holder and transfer the rem 36 (38, 40) sts to ndl. Attach yarn and k32 (34, 36), k2tog, k2. Turn and purl back. With

Pattern 21

RS facing, work a decrease row: k to last 4 sts, k2tog, k2; then work 3 rows in st st. Repeat these 4 rows 10 (12, 12) times until 24 (24, 26) sts remain and 46 (50, 54) rows are worked from armhole. Work even for 4 (4, 2) rows or the same number of rows as for the right front.

Shoulders
With WS facing, put 24 (24, 26) sts back left shoulder sts on a ndl. Hold the back and front left shoulders together (RS facing each other) and use a 3-needle bind-off to join the left shoulder. Rep for the right front and back shoulder sts, using the 24" strand as the working yarn. The center 24 (28, 28) back sts remain on a stitch holder.

Sleeves
Beginning at the right edge of the live armhole sts, with RS facing, place the last 4 st on the smaller circ ndl. Pick up 80 (84, 86) sts (approx 3 sts for every 4 rows) around the armhole and then the

four remaining live sts (88, 92, 94 sts). Be sure to include a st in the "corner" beside the live sts at the bottom of the sleeve. Pm and knit one rnd, transitioning to the larger ndl. Shape sleeves with short rows as follows:

Row 1: k56 (61, 63) sts wrap next st, turn
Row 2: sl 1, p24 (30, 32) sts, wrap, turn
Row 3: sl 1, k26 (32, 34) sts, wrap, turn
Row 4: sl 1, p28 (34, 36) sts, wrap, turn
Row 5: sl 1, k31 (37, 39) sts, wrap, turn
Row 6: sl 1, p34 (40, 42) sts, wrap, turn
Row 7: sl 1, k37 (43, 45) sts, wrap, turn
Row 8: sl 1, p40 (46, 48) sts, wrap, turn
Row 9: sl 1, k43 (49, 51) sts, wrap, turn
Row 10: sl 1, p46 (52, 54) sts, wrap, turn
Row 11: sl 1, k49 (55, 57) sts, wrap, turn
Row 12: sl 1, p53 (58, 60) sts, wrap, turn
Row 13: sl 1, k0 (61, 63) sts, wrap, turn
Row 14: sl 1, P0 (64,66) sts, wrap, turn
Row 15: sl 1, knit to end

Working again in the rnd, work 1 decrease rnd (k2, k2tog, knit to last 4 st in rnd, ssk, k2), then knit 4 rnds even. Repeat these 5 rnds 4 (6, 5) times until 78 (78, 82) sts remain. Work 1 decrease rnd, then knit 3 rnds even. Work these 4 rows 15 (13, 15) times until 46 (50, 50) sts remain. Work 1 (2, 2) more decrease rnds (44, 46, 46 sts) or until sleeve length is 17 (17½, 18)" or 1¾ (2, 2)" shorter than desired length. With smaller ndl, work k2, p2 rib for 12 (14, 14) rnds. Bind off (a sewn bind-off provides maximum elasticity).

Shawl collar
With smaller ndl and RS facing, pick up 98 (102, 106) sts from the bottom of the right front edge (approx 4 st every 5 rows). About 50 (54, 56) sts should be between the lower edge and the first neckline decrease; the last st should be in the shoulder seam. Include one st in the "corner" between the shoulder and neck sts. Place the neck sts on an empty ndl and knit across. Pick up one st in the other "corner" between the neck st and the shoulder (26, 30, 30 sts). Pick up 98 (102, 106) sts along the left front edge, with the first st in the shoulder seam (222, 234, 242 sts total). Turn. Work p2, k2 rib across to end of right band, ending with p2

Begin short row shaping for shawl collar. With RS facing, work in established rib pattern across right band and back neck (31, 33, 34) times. Wrap next stitch (shoulder seam). Turn. Continue shaping as follows:
Row 1 (WS): sl 1, work rib 31 (35, 35) sts, wrap, turn
Row 2 (RS): sl 1, work rib 36 (40, 40) sts, wrap, turn
Row 3: sl 1, work rib 41 (45, 45) sts, wrap, turn
Row 4: sl 1, work rib 46 (50, 50) sts, wrap, turn
Continue working back and forth adding 5 more stitches with each row until there are 111 (125, 125) sts worked from the wrong side, not counting the first slipped stitch. End RS row: sl 1, work rib to end of left band.

Ribbed front bands and buttonholes
Work 2 rows in established rib pattern; end ready to work a WS row. From the right band edge, count up 66 (66, 74) sts and pm to identify the top buttonhole st. From the opposite end of the band, p2, k2 until the marker is reached. Work buttonhole rows as follows:

Buttonhole placement for S/M
1. *(p2, k2) 4 times, slip second st on right ndl over new st and off ndl, (p2, k2). Rep from * 3 times, end p2.
2. *k2, p1, yo, (k2, p2) 3 times. Repeat from * 3 times, work in rib to end.

Buttonhole placement for L
1. *(p2, k2) 4 times, p2, slip second st on right ndl over new st and off, (k2, p2) 4 times, k2, slip second st on right ndl over new st and off. Rep from * once, end p2.
2. k2, *p1, yo. (k2, p2) 4 times, k1, yo (p2, k2) 4 times. Rep from * once. Work rib to end.

Work 4 rows in established rib pattern; end ready to work a RS row. Bind off using a purl stitch from the right side (shown with a decrease bind-off for maximum elasticity). Do not cut yarn.

Bottom band
Using smaller ndl, with WS facing and bottom edge up, take last loop from front bands and pull it through the bottom of the original st to turn corner and create first st in the lower ribbing. Return the stitch to other ndl, then knit the st. Work 7 (8, 8) sts in the front band in this manner and knit them. Remove provisional cast-on and transfer the live sts to the smaller ndl, working from left to right, then knit across. Pick up and knit 8 (9, 9) sts in the bottom of the opposite side of the front band (170, 178, 186 st total). Work 2 rows of k2, p2 rib, beginning with p2 on WS. Work a buttonhole role (WS) as follows: p2, make a one-row buttonhole, work in established rib to end. Work 7 rows even, then work a second buttonhole row. Work 4 rows in established rib, ending ready for a right side row. Bind off in purl (shown with a decrease bind off). Sew on buttons.

One-row buttonhole
1. Sl 1 knitwise. Bring the yarn forward and drop it. Slip the next st knitwise and pass the first slipped st over the second slipped st and off the ndl.
2. Leave the working yarn dropped and bind off 3 more sts in this manner (4 total).
3. Slip the last st on the right hand ndl back to the left ndl. Turn.
4. Bring the working yarn back to the front. Using a purlwise cable cast-on, create 5 new sts. Pass yarn to back. Turn.
5. Slip the first st knitwise onto the right ndl. Slip the second st over the first and off the ndl. Pass yarn to back and slip the first st from the right to the left ndl. One buttonhole completed.

Variation: Garter Stitch Front Bands and Buttonholes

Materials
5 (5, 6) skeins, # 8892 (Azure)

Directions
Work as in main pattern, replacing the ribbed front bands and buttonholes with the following:
Knit 5 rows; end ready to work a RS row. Work appropriate buttonhole row. Finish by working 3 rows in garter st. Bind off using a purl st from the right side. Do not clip working yarn. Work Bottom Band as described in the main pattern.

Buttonhole row for size S:
K3, (make a one-row buttonhole, k10) 3 times, make last buttonhole (this one is positioned just below beginning of neck increases), knit to end of row.

Buttonhole row for size M:
K4, (make a one-row buttonhole, k11) 3 times, make last buttonhole, knit to end of row.

Buttonhole row for size L:
K3, (make a one-row buttonhole, k12) 3 times, make last buttonhole, knit to end of row.

Variation: Double Seed Stitch Folded Cuffs

Materials
6,(6,7) skeins, #9430 (Highland Green)

Double Seed Stitch
Rnds 1 and 2: *k2, p2. Rep from *
Rnds 3 and 4: *p2, k2. Rep from *

Directions
Work as in main pattern through sleeve shaping, until sleeve length is 1¾ (2, 2)" shorter than desired length. Purl 1 rnd to create a fold line. For size L, inc 2 st on this rnd. Knit cuff in double seed st to desired length. Knit one rnd, then bind off in purl.

Drawstring Handbags
design by Urban Tribal Wear Designs

Finished size
10" tall, plus strap

Gauge
5.5 sts x 7 rows = 1"

Materials
1 skein in #8422 (Teal; Color 1)
1 skein in #8910 (Citron; Color 2)
1 skein in #8420 (Purple; Color 3)
US 7 (4.5 mm) 16" circ ndl
Set of US 7 dpn

Seed Stitch (worked in the round)
Rnd 1: *k1, p1; rep from *
Rnd 2: *p1, k1; rep from *

Directions
Using Color 1 and circ ndl, CO 2 sts to start the points at the top of the bag. *Turn, knit into the front and back of the first st, k to end of row. Rep from * until there are 10 sts. Break yarn, leaving a tail long enough to weave in later, and leave the triangle on the ndl. Rep until 8 triangles are made (80 sts).

Begin working in the rnd, knitting all the triangles together. Knit 7 rnds. Work eyelet rnd for drawstring as follows: k2, *yo, ssk, k2, k2tog, yo, k4, rep from *; end with k2. Knit 2 rnds, then change to Color 2 and work in seed st for 6 rnds.

With Color 1 and Color 3, work Chart A for 1 rnd. Knit 4 rnds with Color 2; knit 3 rnds with Color 3. Work Chart B for 1 rnd. Knit 3 rnds with Color 1; knit 2 rnds with Color 2. Work Bobble rnd: *k4, make bobble (k in front, back, and front of first st, turn, p3, turn, k3, turn, p3, slip 1, k2tog, psso), rep from * to end of rnd. Knit 2 rnds with Color 2. Work 6 rnds in seed st using Color 3. Knit 3 rnds with Color 1. Purl 1 rnd with Color 1.

Shape bottom of bag as follows:
Rnd 1: *k8, k2tog, rep from * to end of rnd
Rnd 2: *k7, k2tog, rep from * to end of rnd
Rnd 3: *k6, k2tog, rep from * to end of rnd
Rnd 4: knit
Rnd 5: *k5, k2tog, rep from * to end of rnd
Rnd 6: *k4, k2tog, rep from * to end of rnd
Rnd 7: knit
Rnd 8: *k3, k2tog, rep from * to end of rnd
Rnd 9: *k2, k2tog, rep from * to end of rnd
Rnd 10: knit
Rnd 11: *k1, k2tog, rep from * to end of rnd
Rnd 12: knit
Rnd 13: *k2tog, rep from * to end of rnd
Rnd 14: *k2 tog, rep from * to end of rnd

Work 2 rounds I-cord with rem sts. Bind off.

Make a 32" piece of I-cord with 3 sts of Color 2. Make a second one with Color 3. Weave the I-cord from Color 2 through the eyelets at the top and knot together. Weave the I-cord from Color 3 through the eyelets in the opposite direction and knot together.

Pattern 24

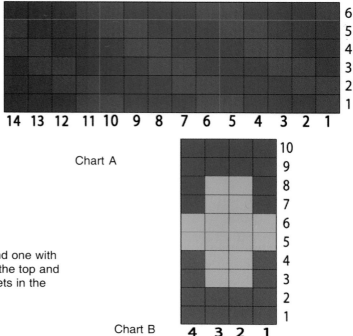

Chart A

Chart B

Variation: Solid color
Materials
3 skeins

Directions
Work as described in the main pattern, replacing Chart A with Chart A2, and replacing Chart B with Chart B2.

Variation: Rolled edge with cable pattern
Materials
3 skeins

5-Stitch Cable
Rnd 1: *c5f, rep from * to the end of the rnd
Rnd 2-4: knit

Directions
CO 80 sts. Pm and join ends, being careful not to twist the circle. Knit 16 rnds. Work eyelet rnd as described in the main pattern. Knit 5 rnds. Work in cable pattern until piece measures 10". Knit 5 rnds. Shape the bottom of the bag and finish as described in the main pattern.

Variation: Lace
Materials
3 skeins

Lace Pattern
Rnd 1: k1, *yo, sl 1, k2tog, psso, k2, yo, k1, rep from * to end
Rnd 2: knit
Rnd 3: k2, *yo, k1, sl 1, k2tog, psso, k1, yo, k3, rep from * to last 7 sts; end yo, k1, sl 1, k2tog, psso, k1, yo, k2
Rnd 4: knit
Rnd 5: k3 *yo, sl 1, k2tog, psso, yo, k5, rep from * to last 6 sts,; end yo, sl 1, k2tog, psso, yo, k3
Rnd 6: knit

CO 80 sts. Pm and join ends, being careful not to twist the circle. Knit 16 rnds. Work eyelet rnd as described in the main pattern. Knit 5 rnds, inc 1 st at the end of last rnd. Work in Lace Pattern until the piece measures 10". Knit 5 rnds, decrease 1 st at end of last rnd. Shape the bottom of the bag and finish as described in the main pattern.

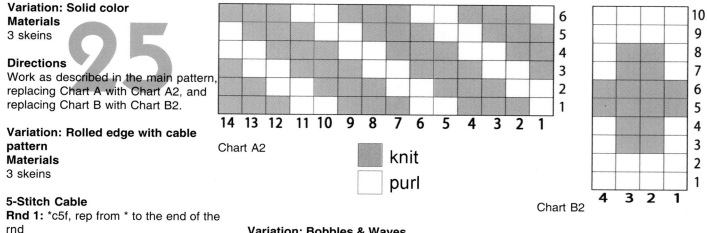

Chart A2

knit
purl

Chart B2

Variation: Bobbles & Waves
Materials
3 skeins

Cable Pattern
Rnd 1: *p2, t3b, p5, c6b, p5, t3f, p2, rep from * to end of rnd
Rnd 2: *p2, k2, p6, k6, p6, k2, p2, rep from * to end of rnd
Rnd 3: *p1, t3b, p4, t5b, p4, t3f, p1, rep from * to end of rnd
Rnd 4: *p1, k2, p5, k3, p4, k3, p5, k2, p1, rep from * to end of rnd
Rnd 5: *t3b, p3, t5b, p4, t4f, p3, t3f, rep from * to end of rnd.
Rnd 6: *k2, p1, make bobble (k in front, back, and front of first st, turn, p3, turn, k3, repeat from * to end of rnd turn, p3, slip 1, k2tog, psso,)p2, k3, p8, k3, p2, make bobble, p1, k2, repeat from * to end of rnd
Rnd 7: *t3f, p3, k3, p8, k3, p3, t3b, rep from * to end of rnd
Rnd 8: *p1, k2, p3, k3, p8, k3, p3, k2, p1, rep from * to end of rnd
Rnd 9: *p1, t3f, p2, t5f, p4, t4b, p2, t3b, p1, rep from * to end of rnd
Rnd 10: *p2, k2, p4, k3, p4, k3, p4, k2, p2, rep from * to end of rnd
Rnd 11: *p2, t3f, p3, t5f, t5b, p3, t3b, p2, rep from * to end of rnd
Rnd 12: *p1, make bobble, p1, k2, p5, k6, p5, k2, p1, make bobble, p1, repeat from * to end of rnd.

Directions
CO 80 sts. Pm and join ends, being careful not to twist the circle. Knit 16 rnds. Work eyelet rnd as described in the main pattern. Knit 5 rnds, dec 2 sts evenly across last round (78 sts). Work Cable Pattern until the piece measures approx 10". Knit 5 rnds, dec 1 st at end of last rnd. Shape bottom of bag and finish as described for the main pattern.

Abbreviations
t3b = sl next st onto cn and hold at back of work, k2 from left ndl, knit sts from cn.
t3f = sl next st onto cn and hold at front of work, k2 from left ndl, knit sts from cn.
t4b = sl next 2 sts onto cn and hold at back of work, k2 from left ndl, then purl sts from cn.
t4f = sl next 2 sts onto cn and hold at front of work, k2 from left ndl, then purl sts from cn.
t5b = sl next 2 sts onto cn and hold at back of work, k3from left ndl, then purl sts from cn.
t5f = sl next 3 sts onto cn and hold at front of work, p2 from left ndl, then knit sts from cn.
c5f: place 3 sts on cn and hold at front of work, k2, k3 from cn.
c6b = sl next 3 sts onto cn and hold at back of work, k3from left ndl, then knit sts from cn.

15

Childs Pullover

design by Urban Tribal Wear Designs

Finished Sizes
Child size 2 (4, 6, 8)
Finished chest measurement 20½ (22, 25, 26½)"

Gauge
5.5 sts x 7 rows = 1" worked in st st

Materials
2 (3, 3, 4) skeins, # 2423 (Montmartre)
US 7 (4.5 mm) ndl
US 6 (4.25 mm) ndl

Directions
Back
With smaller ndl, CO 56 (60, 68, 72) sts. Work in st st for 1". Change to larger ndl and continue in st st until piece measures 7 (8½, 9, 10½)". Place marker for underarm and continue working until piece measures 12 (14½, 15½, 17½)".

Shape shoulders
Bind off 10 (9, 13, 14) sts at beg of next 2 rows. Work 36 (42, 42, 44) back neck sts in st st until funnel neck measures 2½ (2½, 2¾, 3)" from beg. Bind off neatly.

Front
Work same as back.

Sleeves
With smaller ndl, CO 34 (38, 42, 44) sts, work in st st for 1½ (2, 2, 2)". Change to larger ndl and work 1 RS row. Work sleeve shaping as follows: inc 1 st on each side every RS row 6 (3, 1, 0) times, then every 4 rows 5 (11, 14, 17) times (56, 66, 72, 78 sts). Continue working in st st until sleeve measures 7". Bind off.

Finishing
Sew front and back tog at shoulder and side seams. Sew sleeves to body, weave in ends.

Variation: Childs Fair Isle Sweater
Materials
1 skein # 2419 (Aster; C1)
1 skein # 8505 (White; C2)
1 skein # 8910 (Citron; C3)
1 skein # 4147 (Lemon Yellow; C4)
1 skein #8834 (Medium Rose; C5)

Directions
Work sweater as described in the main pattern, following Chart A. Work bobble as follows: knit in the front, back, and front of the next st. Turn. P3, turn, k3,

Pattern 32

turn, p3, turn, sl 1, k2tog, psso. Bobble complete. Finish as described in main pattern.

Variation: Striped Childs Sweater
Materials
5 colors as listed for Fair Isle Sweater

Directions
Work sweater as described in the main pattern. Work stripes as follows, repeating throughout:
Row 1-10: C1
Rows 11-14: C2
Row 15: C3
Row 16-22: C4
Row 23-25: C5
Row 26-30: C2
Row 31-34: C4
Row 35: C1
Row 36-44: C5

Variation: Textured Childs Sweater
Materials
2 (3, 3, 3) skeins, # 7824

Directions
Work sweater as described in main pattern, following Chart B. Finish as described in main pattern.

Variation: Childs Sweater with Graphic Patch Pocket
Materials
2 (3, 3, 4) skeins, # 2423 (Montmartre; sweater main color)
Small amount of # 8914 (Granny Smith; pocket main color)
Small amount of # 7815 ((Summer Sky; pocket contrast color)
Small amount of # 8686 (Brown; pocket contrast color)

Directions
With smaller ndl, CO 56 (60, 68, 72) sts with pocket contrast color. Work in st st for 1". Change to larger ndl and sweater main color and continue as described in main sweater pattern. Work last inch of funnel neck and the first inch of sleeves in pocket main color.

Pockets
Make 2 pockets, following Chart C. Center pocket on front of sweater and sew in place. Reinforce the top corners with a few extra stitches for durability.

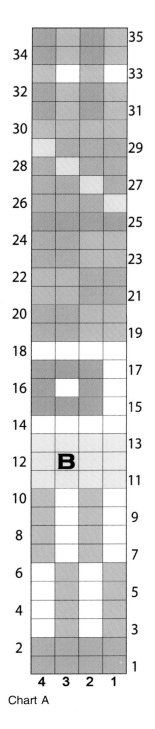

Chart A

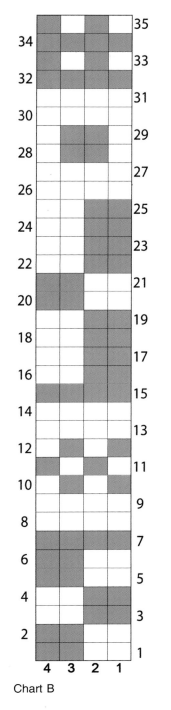

Chart B

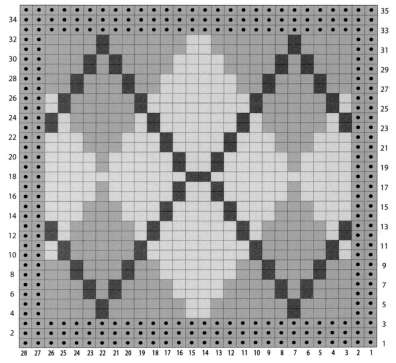

Chart C

● knit on both right and wrong side

▨ knit on right side, purl on wrong side
☐ purl on right side, knit on wrong side
B bobble: knit in the front, back,
and front of the next st. turn.
p3, turn, k3, turn, p3, turn,
sl 1, k2tog, psso, resume pattern

17

Funky Origami Slippers

design by Urban Tribal Wear Designs

Finished Sizes
Toddler (child, woman, man)

Gauge
5.5 sts x 7 rows = 1" worked in st st

Materials
3 skeins, #9433 (Quatro)
US 7 (4.5 mm) ndl
US 6 (4.25 mm) dpn
12" piece of ribbon

Directions
Note: to work increase rows, inc 1 st by knitting into the front and back of first st, work to the end of the row. To work dec rows, knit the first 2 sts tog (RS) or purl the first 2 sts tog (WS), work to the end of the row.

Section 1
CO 2 sts. Working in st st, work inc rows until side 2 of the piece measures 2¼ (2¾, 3¼, 3¾)". Begin working dec rows until only 2 sts remain.

Section 2
Working in st st, work inc rows until side 1 and 2 measures 4½ (5½, 9½, 11)". Begin working dec rows until side 7 measures 2¼ (2¾, 3¼, 3¾)". See diagram on page 19.

Section 3
Work increase rows until side 7 measures 2¼ (2¾, 3¼, 3¾)". Work half of the sts, turn. Working back and forth on half of the sts, work dec rows until only 2 sts remain. Bind off. Reattach yarn and work dec rows back and forth on rem sts until only 2 sts rem. Bind off. Stitch corresponding sides together as shown on diagram: section 1 to 1, section 2 to 2, etc. When all sections are stitched, secure the heel point (that sticks out if you put the slipper on) to the top center of the heel creating a loop. You may attach a bell, bow, pom-pom or leave plain as a cushion for the foot.

Eyelets and Ruffle
With dpns and RS facing, pick up an even number of sts around the top opening. Turn. Work back and forth in k1, p1 ribbing for 4 rows. Work eyelet row as follows: k2, yo, k2tog, work in rib to last 4 sts, k2tog, yo, k2. Work 3 rows in k1, p1 ribbing. Repeat these 4 rows once (2 eyelets on each side).

Work ruffle as follows:
Row 1: *k in front and back of next st, purl, rep from *
Row 2: *k1, p2, rep from *
Row 3: *k1, k in front and back of next st, purl, rep from *
Row 4: *k1, p3, rep from *
Row 5: *k3, p1, rep from *

Rep row 4 and 5 twice. Bind off loosely in k3, p1 pattern. Lace a piece of ribbon into eyelets.

Variation: Two-Color Origami Slipper
Materials
2 skein (Color 1)
1 skein (Color 2)

Seed Stitch
Row 1: *k1, p1; rep from *, end k1.
Row 2: knit the purl sts and purl the knit sts.

Directions
Work slipper as described in the main pattern. Work Section 1 with Color 1 in seed st. Work Section 2 with Color 2 in st st. Work Section 3 with Color 1 in seed st. Work cuff in Color 2. Finish as described in the main pattern.

Variation: Striped Origami Slipper
Materials
2 skein (Color 1)
1 skein (Color 2)

Directions
Work slipper as described in the main pattern, working 2 rows in Color 1 and 2 rows in Color 2 throughout, carrying the yarn up the sides. Finish as described in the main pattern.

Variation: Embroidered Slipper
Materials
3 skeins
small amount for contrasting color

Directions
Work slipper as described in the main pattern. Before finishing, use a a contrasting color to embroider a diamond spiral on the toe piece.

Cuff
Pick up an even number of sts. Join, being careful not to twist the circle, and work in k1, p1 rib until cuff measures 6 (8, 9, 10)". Work 2 rnds in contrast color. Bind off loosely.

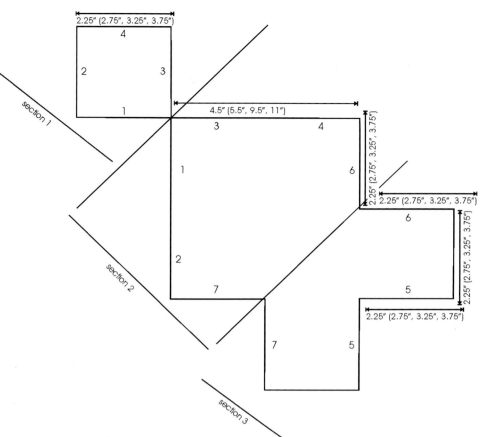

Variation: Seed Stitch Origami Slippers
Materials
3 skeins
3 or 4 buttons for each slipper

Seed Stitch
Row 1: *k1, p1; rep from *, end k1.
Row 2: knit the purl sts and purl the knit sts.

Directions
Work slipper as in main pattern until cuff. Work cuff back and forth in k1, p1 rib for 4 rows. Add 2 (2, 3, 3) eyelet buttonholes as described in main pattern, but only on one side. Continue k1, p1 rib for 4 rows beyond top button hole. Bind off loosely and attach buttons. Or instead of buttonholes, you can use a brooch, a pin or stitch a button in place.

Spiral Rib Hat

design by Mary Lou Egan

Finished Sizes
Child S (M, L) 19(20½, 21½)"
Adult S/M (22½"), M/L (24")

Materials
1 skein, #8407 (Oyster)
US 5 (3.75 mm) 16" (40 cm) circ ndl
US 7 (4.5 mm) 16" circ ndl, or size to obtain gauge
US 7 dpn, or size to match larger ndls

Gauge
5 st = 1" worked in st st in the round on larger needles

Directions
Cuff
With larger circ ndl, CO 96, (100, 108, 112, 120) sts. Pm and join ends, being careful not to twist the circle. Switch to smaller ndl and work k2, p2 rib for 3 (3, 3, 4, 4)". For sizes Childs M, and Adult S/M increase 2 sts in the final round of cuff.

Pattern 39

Head
Switch to larger ndls.
Rnd 1-6: *k3, p3, rep from *
Rnd 7-12: p1, *k3, p3, rep from*, end p2
Rnd 13-18: p2, *k3, p3, rep from*, end p1

Continue in this way, moving the rib one st from the marker every 7th rnd. When hat measures 7, (7½, 8, 8½, 9)" from the beginning, begin decrease rnds. If you are not at the beginning of rnd 1, move the marker to the first set of k3 in the rnd. This will be the new beginning of the rnd. When the sts no longer fit comfortably around the ndl, switch to dpn.

Decrease for top
Rnd 1: *k3, p3, k2, ssk, p2.; rep from *
Rnd 2:   work as established
Rnd 3: *k2, ssk, p2, k3, p2; rep from *
Rnd 4: *k3, p2, k3, p2; rep from *
Rnd 5: *k1, ssk, p2, k3, p2; rep from *
Rnd 6: *k2, p2, k3, p2; rep from *
Rnd 7: p1, *k2, p2, k1, ssk, p2; rep from *, end p1
Rnd 8: p1, *k2, p2; repeat from *, end p1
Rnd 9: p1*k1, ssk, p1, k2, p2; rep from *, end p1
Rnd 10: p1, *k2, p1, k1, ssk, p1; rep from *, end ssk
Rnd 11: p1, *ssk, p1, k2, p1; rep from *, end k2
Rnd 12: p1, *k1, p1, ssk, p1; rep from *, end ssk
Rnd 13: p1, *k1, p1, ssk; rep from *, end k1, move marker 1 st
Rnd 14: *ssk, k1, ssk, k1, ssk, k1
Rnd 15: ssk across rnd

Cut yarn, leaving about 6" for a finishing strand. Draw strand through sts left on ndl, and weave in ends.

Inset Shrugs

design by Patti Pierce Stone

Finished sizes
S/M, (L/XL)
Sleeve edge to sleeve edge: 66½ (73)"
Cuff: 5¾ (6¾)"
Body opening: 26½ (31)"

Gauge
24 sts x 30 rows = 4" worked in st st

Materials
5(6) skeins, #4010 (Straw)
US 4 (3.5mm) 24" (60 cm) circ ndl

Ribbing
K1, [p1, k2] 6 (7) times, p1, k1, [p1, k2] 6 (7) times, p1, k1

Squiggle Lace
Right Lace Edge
Rnd 1 (RS): k1, p1, k2tog, yo, p1, k1, p1, k2tog, yo, p1
Rnd 2: k1, p1, k2, p1, k1, p1, k2, p1
Rnd 3: k1, p1, yo, ssk, p1, k1, p1, yo, ssk, p1
Rnd 4: k1, p1, k2, p1, k1, p1, k2, p1
Rnd 5-8: Rep Rnd 1-4.

Center Lace
Rnd 1 (RS): p1, k2tog, yo, p1, k1,p1, k2tog, yo, p1, k1, p1, yo, ssk, p1, k1, p1, yo, ssk, p1
Rnd 2: p1, k2, p1, k1, p1, k2, p1, k1, p1, k2, p1, k1, p1, k2, p1
Rnd 3: p1, yo, ssk, p1, k1, p1, yo, ssk, p1, k1, p1, k2tog, yo, p1, k1, p1, k2tog, yo, p1
Rnd 4: p1, k2, p1, k1, p1, k2, p1, k1, p1, k2, p1, k1, p1, k2, p1
Rnd 5-8: Rep Rnd 1-4.

Left Lace Edge
Rnd 1 (RS): k1, p1, yo, ssk, p1, k1, p1, yo, ssk, p1.
Rnd 2: k1, p1, k2, p1, k1, p1, k2, p1.
Rnd 3: k1, p1, k2tog, yo, p1, k1, p1, k2tog, yo, p1.
Rnd 4: k1, p1, k2, p1, k1, p1, k2, p1.
Rnd 5-8: Rep Rnd 1-4.

Inc-L: make a lifted inc in the st 1 row below the one just worked by knitting in the left leg of that st.
Inc-R: make a lifted inc in the next st in the row below the current row by knitting in the right leg of the st.

Directions
CO 41(47) sts with a long-tail cast on and join to form a circle. Work 14 rnds in ribbing. Work a transition row as follows:

Pattern 40

k1, p1, k2, p1, k1, p1, k2, inc-R, k1, [p1, k2] 3 (4) times, k1, p1, [p1, k2] 3(4) times, p1, k1, inc-L, k2, p1, k1, p1, k2, p1, k1 (43, 49 sts).

Cuff to Elbow
Establish patterning as follows: work Right Lace Edge, pm, k2 (5), pm, work Center Lace, pm, k2 (5), pm, work Left Lace Edge.

Work an inc rnd as follows: work rnd 2 of Right Lace Edge, inc-r, k2 (5), inc-L, work rnd 2 of Center Lace, inc-r, k2 (5), inc-l, work rnd 2 of Left Lace Edge (47, 53 sts). Beg with rnd 3 of stitch patterns, work lace patterns 7 (8) times. Rep the inc each time you work rnd 2, the inc made after the first marker and before the second marker, after the third marker and before the fourth marker (75, 85 sts).

Elbow to Shoulder
Work 4 (5) lace pattern repeats (or until work measures approx 6" from shoulder) without inc. End with rnd 8. Then begin working an inc rnd on each rnd 2 and rnd 6, working 3 (4) more pattern rep (99, 117 sts). Then work an inc rnd on each rnd 2, 4, 6, and 8, working 2 pattern rep (131, 149 sts). Work one more pattern

rep, but increase only between the first 2 markers on rnds 2, 4, 6, and 8 (139, 157 sts).

Back (worked back and forth)
Note: to adapt stitch patterns for flat knitting, work RS rows as written. When WS is facing, purl all sts that resemble purl sts, knit all yo and all sts that resemble knit sts.

Work 24 (28) lace pattern rep, or until back measures 26½ (31)" from opening. End after row 1. Join circle and begin knitting again in the rnd.

Shoulder to Elbow
Beg with rnd 2, work one lace pattern rep with the following dec on rnds 2, 4, 6, and 8: k2tog after the first marker and ssk the

2 sts before the second marker (131, 149 sts). Work lace pattern 2 more times, working the following dec on each rnd 2, 4, 6, and 8: k2tog after first marker, ssk before second marker, k2tog after third marker, ssk with last 2 sts before the fourth marker (99, 117 sts). Rep lace pattern 3(4) more times working the 4-st decreases in rnd 2 and 6 only (75, 85 sts).

Elbow to Cuff
Work 4 (5) pattern rep without dec. Then work 7 (8) pattern rep, dec 4 sts on each rnd 2 (47, 53 sts). Work rnds 1 – 3, working dec on rnd 2 (43, 49 sts).

Work transition rnd: k1, p1, k2, p1, k1, p1, k1, k2tog, k1, [p1, k2] 3 (4) times, k1, p1, [k2, p1] 3(4) times, k1, ssk, k1, p1, k1, p1, k2, p1, k1 (41, 47 sts). Work rib for 14 rnds. Bind off with a sewn bind-off so that the cast-on and bind-off edges match.

Finishing
Pick up sts in the edge around the center opening (between the sleeves), approx 4 sts for every 5 rows. (153, 180 sts). Work around in k2, p1 rib for 1 ½". Bind off with an elastic edge as follows: *bind off 2 sts, cast on 1, rep from * around.

Variation: Stockinette Shrug with Eyelets
Materials
5(6) skeins, #9422 (Tibetan Rose)

Eyelet Lace
Right Edge
Rnd 1: k1, p1, k2tog, yo, k3, yo, ssk, p1
Rnd 2: p1, k1, p7, p1
Rnd 3-8: rep rnd 1-2

Center
Rnd 1: k1, p1, k2tog, yo, k3, yo, ssk, k1, k2tog, yo, k3, yo, ssk, p1, k1.
Rnd 2: p1, k1, p15, k1, p1.
Rnd 3-8: rep rnd 1-2

Left Edge
Rnd 1: k1, p1, k2tog, yo, k3, yo, ssk, p1.
Rnd 2: p1, k1, p7, p1.
Rnd 3-8: rep rnd 1-2

Directions
Work shrug as described in main pattern, substituting Eyelet Lace for the Squiggle Lace pattern.

Ascot Scarves
design by Patti Pierce Stone

Finished Size
About 34"

Materials
1 skein, #8234 (Pistachio)
US 7 (4.5 mm) ndl
Set of US 7 dpn

Gauge
1.5" x 4.75" (blocked) worked in Faux Cable pattern (1 repeat)

Faux Cable Pattern
Note: slip all stitches as if to purl
Row 1 (RS): k to marker, p1, yo, k3, ssk, k3, p1, k to last 2 st, sl 2 wyif
Row 2/4/6/8: k4, p to marker, k1, p8, k1, p to last 4 st, k2, sl 2 wyif
Row 3: k to marker, p1, k1, yo, k3, ssk, k2, p1, k to last 2 st, sl 2 wyif
Row 5: k to marker, p1, k2, yo, k3, ssk, k1, p1, k to last 2 sts, sl 2 wyif
Row 7: k to marker, p1, k3, yo, k3, ssk, p1, k to last 2 st, sl 2 wyif
Row 9: k to marker, p1, k8, p1, k to last 2 st, sl 2 wyif
Row 10: k4, p to marker, k1, p8, k1, p to last 4 st, k2, sl 2 wyif

Directions
CO 12 st using a cable cast-on method.

Begin increases
Rows 1– 4: k2, m1, k to last 2 st, sl 2 wyif (16 sts)
Row 5 (RS): k2, m1, k1, pm, p1, yo, k3, ssk, k3, p1, k to last 2 st, sl 2 wyif (17 sts)
Row 6: k2, m1, k1, pm, k1, p8, k1, p to last 3 st, k1, sl 2 wyif (18 sts)
Row 7: k2, m1, k to marker, p1, k1, yo, k3, ssk, k2, p1, k to last 3 st, k1, sl 2 wyif (19 sts)
Rows 8/10/12: k2, m1, k1, p to marker, k1, p8, k1, p to last 3 st, k1, sl 2 wyif (20/22/24 sts)
Row 9: k2, m1, k to marker, p1, k2, yo, k3, ssk, k1, p1, k to last 2 st, sl 2 wyif (21 sts)
Row 11: k2, m1, k to marker, p1, k3, yo, k3, ssk, p1, k to last 2 st, sl 2 wyif (23 sts)
Row 13: k2, m1, k to marker, p1, k8, p1, k to last 2 st, sl 2 wyif (25 sts)
Row 14: k2, m1, k1, p to marker, k1, p8, k1, p to last 3 st, k1, sl 2 wyif (26 sts)

Pattern 42

With 26 sts on ndl, work rows 1 – 10 of Faux Cable Pattern twice, then work rows 1 – 9 again for a total of 29 rows (6¼" from cast-on edge).

Begin Keyhole

With RS facing and holding 2 dpn parallel, transfer the first st to front dpn, then alternate st between back and front dpn, placing last 2 sts on front dpn (14 sts front, 12 sts back). Place sts on back dpn onto a stitch holder or piece of waste yarn. Each set of sts will be worked separately. Work Keyhole Front twice (16 rows). Then put front keyhole sts onto a stitch holder and place the back keyhole sts onto the working ndl. Attach new yarn and work Keyhole Back 7 times (14 rows).

Keyhole Front
Row 1/3/5/7 (WS): k3, p8, k1, sl 2 wyif
Row 2: k2, p1, yo, k3, ssk, k3, p1, sl 2 wyif
Row 4: k2, p1, k1, yo, k3, ssk, k2, p1, sl 2 wyif
Row 6: k2, p1, k2, yo, k3, ssk, k1, p1, sl 2 wyif
Row 8: k2, p1, k3, yo, k3, ssk, p1, sl 2 wyif

Keyhole Back
Row 1 (WS): k4, p4, k2, sl 2 wyif
Row 2: k2, p2, k4, p2, sl 2 wyif

With WS facing, join front and back keyhole sts by transferring the first 2 sts from the front keyhole ndl, then first st from back keyhole ndl onto working ndls. Alternate transferring 1st from front and back ndls.

Neckpiece
Work transition row: k4, p4, pm, k1, p8, k1, pm, p to last 4 st. k2, sl 2 wyif. Then work row 1-10 of Faux Cable Pattern 16 times.

Begin decreases
Row 1 (RS): k2, ssk, k to marker, p1, yo, k3, ssk, k3, p1, k to last 2 st, sl 2 wyif (25 sts)
Row 2/4/6/8: k2, ssk, k1, p to marker, k1, p8, k1, p to last 4 st, k2, sl 2 wyif (24/22/20/18 sts)
Row 3: k2, ssk, k to marker, p1, k1, yo, k3, ssk, k2, p1, k to last 2 st, sl 2 wyif (23 sts)
Row 5: k2, ssk, k to marker, p1, k2, yo, k3, ssk, k1, p1, k to last 2 st, sl 2 wyif (21 sts)
Row 7: k2, ssk, k to marker, p1, k3, yo, k3, ssk, p1, k to last 2 st, sl 2 wyif (19 sts)
Row 9: k2, ssk, p1, k8, p1, k to last 2 st, sl 2 wyif (17 sts)
Row 10: k2, ssk, k to last 2 st, sl 2 wyif (16 sts)

Finishing
Row 1 (RS): k2, ssk, k to last 2 st, sl 2 wyif (15 sts)
Row 2: k2, ssk, k to last 2 st, sl 2 wyif (14 sts)
Repeat rows 1 and 2 (12 sts). Bind off.

Variation: Lacy Keyhole Scarf
Materials
1 skein, #8505 (white)

Gauge
10 st x 12 rows = 2" worked in st st

Stockinette and I-Cord
Note: slip all stitches as if to purl
Row 1 (RS): k to last 2 st, sl 2 wyif
Row 2: k4, p to last 4 st, k2, sl 2 wyif

Directions
CO 12 st using a cable cast-on method.

Begin increases
Rows 1 – 4: k2, m1, k to last 2 st, sl 2 wyif (16 sts)

Row 5: k2, m1, k1, [yo, ssk] 5 times, k1, sl 2 wyif (17 sts)
Row 6/8/10: k2, m1, p to last 3 st, k1, sl 2 wyif (18/20/22 sts)
Row 7: k2, m1, k1, [yo, ssk] 6 times, k1, sl 2 wyif (19 sts)
Row 9: k2, m1, k1, [yo, ssk] 7 times, k1, sl 2 wyif (21 sts)
Row 11: k2, m1, k1, [yo, ssk] 8 times, k1, sl 2 wyif (23 sts)
Row 12: k2, m1, p to last 3 st, k1, sl 2 wyif (24 sts)

Work Stockinette and I-Cord pattern 14 times, then work row 1 again for a total of 29 rows (6¼" from cast-on edge).

Begin keyhole
Divide sts into front (13 sts) and back (11 sts) keyhole as described in the main pattern. Work Keyhole Front 4 times (16 rows). Then put front keyhole sts onto a stitch holder, and place the back keyhole sts onto the working ndls. Attach new yarn and work Keyhole Back 7 times (14 rows).

Keyhole Front
Row 1/3 (WS): k2, p to last 2 st, sl 2 wyif
Row 2: k2, [yo, ssk] 4 times, k1, sl 2 wyif
Row 4: k2, k1, [yo, ssk] 4 times, sl 2 wyif

Keyhole back
Row 1: k3, (p1, k1) to last 2 st, sl 2 wyif
Row 2: k2, (p1, k1) to last 2 st, sl 2 wyif

With WS facing, join front and back keyhole sts as described in the main pattern. Work Stockinette and I-Cord pattern, beginning with row 2, until piece measures 24 in from end of keyhole. End with row 2.

Pattern 43

Pattern 44

Begin decreases
Row 1: k2, ssk, [yo, ssk] 8 times, k2, sl 2 wyif. (23 sts)
Row 2/4/6 (WS): k2, ssk, p to last 3 st, k1, sl 2 wyif (22/20/18 sts)
Row 3: k2, ssk, [yo, ssk] 7 times, k2, sl 2 wyif. (21 sts)
Row 5: k2, ssk, [yo, ssk] 6 times, k2, sl 2 wyif. (19 sts)
Row 7: k2, ssk, [yo, ssk] 5 times, k2, sl 2 wyif. (17 sts)
Row 8: k2, ssk, k to last 2 st, sl 2 wyif. (16 sts)

Finish as described in main pattern.

Variation: Beaded Keyhole Scarf
Materials
1 skein, #7810 (Amethyst)
100 6/0 beads

Directions
Thread beads onto yarn. CO 12 sts using a cable cast-on method.

Begin increases
Rows 1 – 4: k2, m1, k to last 2 st, sl 2 wyif (16 sts)
Row 5: k2, m1, [k1, sl 1 with bead in front] 5 times, k2, sl 2 wyif (17 sts)
Row 6/8/10: k2, m1, p to last 3 st, k1, sl 2 wyif (18/20/22 sts)
Row 7: k2, m1, [sl 1 with bead in front, k1] 7 times, sl 2 wyif (19 sts)
Row 9: k2, m1, [k1, sl 1 with bead in front] 7 times, k2, sl 2 wyif (21 sts)
Row 11: k2, m1, [sl 1 with bead in front, k1] 9 times, sl 2 wyif (23 sts)
Row 12: k2, m1, p to last 3 st, k1, sl 2 wyif (24 sts)

Work Stockinette and I-Cord pattern (see Lacy Keyhole Scarf) 14 times, then work row 1 again for a total of 29 rows (6¼" from cast-on edge).

Begin keyhole
Divide sts into front (13 sts) and back (11 sts) keyhole as described in main pattern. Work Keyhole Front 4 times (16 rows). Put front keyhole sts onto a stitch holder and place the back keyhole st back onto working needles. Attach new yarn and work Keyhole Back 7 times (14 rows).

Keyhole Front
Row 1/3 (WS): k2, p to last 2 st, sl 2 wyif
Row 2: k2, [k1, sl 1 with bead in front] 4 times, k1, sl 2 wyif
Row 4: k2, k1, [k1, sl 1 with bead in front] 4 times, sl 2 wyif

Keyhole Back
Row 1: k3, (p1, k1) to last 2 st, sl 2 wyif
Row 2: k2, (p1, k1) to last 2 st, sl 2 wyif

With WS facing, join front and back keyhole sts as described in main pattern. Work Stockinette and I-Cord pattern, beginning with row 2, until piece measures 24" from end of keyhole. End after row 2.

Begin decreases
Row 1 (RS): k2, ssk, [sl 1 with bead in front, k1] 9 times, sl 2 wyif (23 sts)
Row 2/4/6: k2, ssk, p to last 3 st, k1, sl wyif (22/20/18 sts)
Row 3: k2, ssk, [k1, sl 1 with bead in front] 7 times, k2, sl 2 wyif (21 sts)
Row 5: k2, ssk, [sl 1 with bead in front, k1] 7 times, k2, sl 2 wyif (19 sts)
Row 7: k2, ssk, [k1, sl 1 with bead in front] 5 times, k2, sl 2 wyif (17 sts)
Row 8: k2, ssk, k to last 2 st, sl 2 wyif (16 sts)

Finish as described in main pattern.

Pattern 45

Variation – Stockinette Keyhole Scarf
Materials
1 skein, #7810 (Amethyst)

Directions
CO 12 sts using a cable cast-on method. Work increases as follows:
Rows 1 – 4: k2, m1, k to last 2 st, sl 2 wyif (16 sts)
Rows 5/7/9/11 (RS): k2, m1, k to last 2 st, sl 2 wyif (17/19/21/23 sts)
Rows 6/8/10/12: k2, m1, p to last 3 st, k1, sl 2 wyif (18/20/22/24 sts)

Work Stockinette and I-Cord pattern (see Lacy Keyhole Scarf) 14 times, then work row 1 again for a total of 29 rows (6¼" from cast-on edge).

Begin keyhole
Divide sts into front (13 sts) and back (11 sts) keyhole as described in main pattern. Work Front Keyhole 8 times (16 rows). Put front keyhole sts onto a stitch holder, and place the back keyhole sts back onto working ndls. Attach new yarn and work Keyhole Back 7 times (14 rows).

Keyhole Front
Row 1 (wrong side): k2, (p1, k1) to last 2 st, sl wyif
Row 2: k3, (P1, k1) to last 2 st, sl wyif

Keyhole Back
Row 1: k3, (p1, k1) to last 2 st, sl 2 wyif
Row 2: k2, (p1, k1) to last 2 st, sl 2 wyif

With WS facing, join front and back keyhole sts as described in main pattern. Work Stockinette and I-Cord pattern, beginning with row 2, until piece measures 24" from end of keyhole. End with row 2.

Begin decreases
Row 1/3/5/7 (RS): k2, ssk, k to last 2 st, sl 2 wyif (23/21/19/17 sts)
Row 2/4/6/8: k2, ssk, p to last 3 st, k1, sl 2 wyif (22/20/18/16 sts)

Finish as described in the main pattern.

23

Rectangle Shrugs
design by Urban Tribal Wear Designs

Finished Sizes
Small (Large)

Materials
7 skeins
US 7 (4.5 mm) ndl, or size to obtain gauge
Gauge for main pattern
5.5 sts x 7 rows = 1"

Seed Stitch (odd number of sts)
Row 1: *k1, p1; rep from *, end k1.
Rep row 1.

Directions
CO 79 sts. Work 2" of seed st for border. Work Chart 1 three times, keeping the first and last 3 sts in seed st for selvedge edge. Continue until the piece measures 56". Work 2" of seed st for border. Bind off in seed st.

Sew seams
Fold the rectangle in half and sew along sleeve seam as shown in Figure 1, leaving 18 (22)" open for the body. Add a fringe along the cuff, if desired.

Variation: Ostrich Lace
This version has a curvy finish along the cuff and edges.

Materials
7 skeins

Ostrich Lace
Row 1 and all other odd-numbered rows (WS): purl.
Rows 2, 6, 10, 14, 18, 22, 26, and 30: knit.
Rows 4, 8, 12, 16: [k1, yo] 3 times, *[ssk] 2 times, sl 2 knitwise, k1, p2sso, [k2 tog] twice, [yo, k1] 5 times, yo; rep from *, end [ssk] 2 times, sl 2 knitwise, k1, p2sso, [k2tog] twice, [yo, k1] 3 times.
Rows 20, 24, 28, 32: [k2 tog] 3 times, *[yo, k1] 5 times, yo, [ssk] twice, sl 2 knitwise, k1, p2sso, [k2 tog] twice; rep from *, end [yo, k1] 5 times, yo, [ssk] 3 times.

Directions
CO 81 sts. Work Ostrich Lace pattern 14 times or until the piece measures approx 60". Bind off. Sew seams as described in the main pattern.

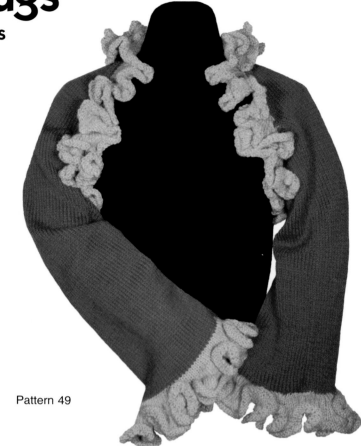

Pattern 49

Variation: Diamond Shrug with Deep Rib Knit Cuffs
Materials
7 skeins
Size 6 (4.25 mm) ndl

Directions
With smaller ndl, CO 44 sts. Work k2, p2 rib until the piece measures 10" (cuffs will be folded back or scrunched up). Change to larger ndl and inc 32 sts evenly across the next row. Keeping the first and last 5 sts in garter stitch (knit all rows) as a selvedge edge, work diamond pattern (Chart 2) until the piece measures 50". Dec 32 sts evenly across next row. Change to smaller ndl and work k2, p2 rib until the cuff measures 10". Bind off. Sew a bead and sequins into the center of each diamond as shown in Figure 3. Sew sleeve seams as described in the main pattern.

Variation: Ruffled Cuff and Edging
Materials
5 skeins #2414(Ginger; MC)
2 skeins #8012 (Doeskin Heather; CC)

Ruffle Pattern
Row 1 (increase row): *K1, m1, repeat to end.
Row 2: Purl
Row 3: Knit
Row 4: Purl

Directions
With MC, CO 78 sts. Work in st st until the piece measures 60". Bind off. With CC, pick up 76 sts along the cuff edge (leaving the first and last st of the cuff for sewing up – the ruffle will not be joined at the edge). Continue in st st for ½", ending with a WS row. Work Ruffle Pattern until the ruffle measures 4". Work 2 rows in st st. Bind off loosely. Rep for second cuff. Sew seams as described in the main pattern.

Using CC with RS facing, pick up an even number of sts all the way around the

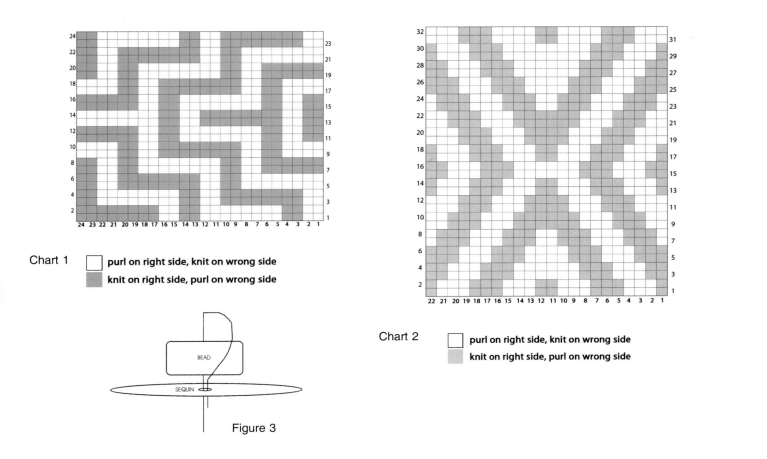

Chart 1

☐ purl on right side, knit on wrong side

▨ knit on right side, purl on wrong side

Figure 3

Chart 2

☐ purl on right side, knit on wrong side

▨ knit on right side, purl on wrong side

body opening. Rep the ruffle pattern around the body opening until the ruffle measures 5". See Figure 2. Work 3 rows in st st. Bind off loosely.

Variation: Flared-Arm Shrug
This one is a little longer so the rolled cuff hangs slightly over the hand.

Materials
3 skeins # 8908 (Anis, Color 1)
2 skeins #8910 (Citron, Color 2)
2 skeins #8686 (Brown, Color 3)
US 6 (4.25 mm) ndl

Directions
With larger ndl and Color 1, CO 80 sts. Work in st st for 6". Change to Color 2 and work in k2, p2 rib for 8". Change to Color 3 and work in st st until the piece measures 50". Change to Color 2 and work in k2, p2 rib for 8". Change to Color 1 and work in st st for 6". Bind off. Sew sleeves as described in the main pattern.

With smaller ndl and Color 2, pick up an even number of stitches around the body opening and work in k1, p1 rib for 2 in. Work 1 row in color 1. Bind off in k1, p1 rib with Color 1 using larger ndl.

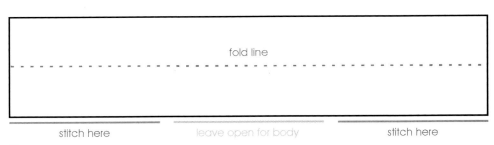

fold line

stitch here   leave open for body   stitch here

Figure 1

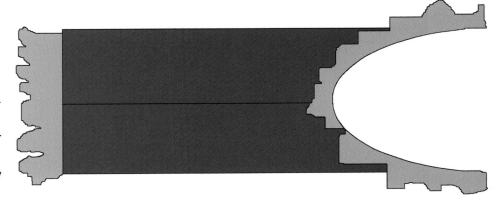

Figure 2 - Half of shrug shown.

25

Jester Hats

design by Urban Tribal Wear Designs

Finished size
Child (Adult S, Adult L) 18 (20, 22)"
Gauge
5.5 sts x 7rows = 1"
Materials
1 skein, #9433 (Quatro)
Set of US 7 (4.5 mm) dpn
Set of US 6 (4.25 mm) dpn

Directions

With smaller ndl, CO 90 (96, 108) sts. Pm and join ends, being careful not to twist the circle. Work in st st for 1". Continue in k2, p1 rib for 2 (2½, 3)". Change to larger ndl and work in st st for 2 (3½, 4½)".
Break yarn, leaving a 12-14" tail for finishing. Place 60 (64, 72) sts on holder or scrap yarn.
Using free dpn, CO 15 (16, 18) sts. Using a second dpn, work 15 (16, 18) sts from working ndl. Using a third dpn, work 15 (16, 18) sts. Pm and join (the cast-on sts are the top of the hat). Decrease for the jester points as follows: dec at the beg and end of each ndl every 4 (5, 6) rnds until only 3 sts remain. Work 3 rnds and then *slip 1, k2tog, psso repeat from * until only 3 sts remain. Work I-cord with rem 3 sts for 2". Bind off. Using tail from I-cord, loop the I-cord back toward the base of the I-cord, creating a loop.

Work the second point as follows: using a free dpn, cast on 15 (16, 18) sts. Using a second dpn, work 15 (16, 18) sts from holder. Using a third dpn, work 15 (16, 18) sts. Pm and join. Decrease jester point as described above. Work a third point in the same way. Sew the top of the hat together as shown in diagram. Weave in loose ends.

Note: For longer points, dec each side of each ndl every 7 (8, 9) rnds. For a "flower look" at the top, dec for longer points every 7 (8, 9) rnds, then secure the I-cord to the base of the point along the outside brim of the hat. You can also embroider around the brim, and add bells or pom-poms to the tips.

Variation: Striped Jester Hat
Materials
2 skeins of different colors

Directions
Work jester hat as described in the main pattern, working 2 rows in Color 1, and 2 rows in Color 2, carrying yarn up the inside.

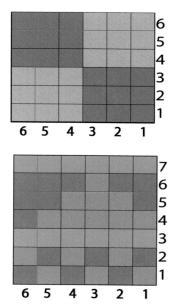

Pattern 51

Variation: 3-Color Intarsia Jester Hat
Materials
3 skeins of different colors

Directions
With Color 1, work jester hat through the 1-in brim as described in the main pattern. Then begin working in intarsia as follows: work ndl 1 with Color 1, ndl 2 with Color 2, and ndl 3 with Color 3. Use the corresponding color with each point.

Variation: 3-Color Jester Hat with Brim
Materials
3 skeins of different colors

Directions
CO with Color 1 as described in the main pattern. Work a k1, p1 ribbing for 5 (7, 8½)". Then begin spiral intarsia in st st for 1 (3½, 4½)" as follows:

Rnd 1: work ndl 1 with Color 1, ndl 2 with Color 2, ndl 3 with Color 3
Rnd 2: on ndl 1, work first st with Color 3, work rem with Color 1; on ndl 2, work first st with Color 1, work rem with Color 2; on ndl 3, work first st with Color 2, work rem with Color 3.
Rnd 3: on ndl 1, work first and second sts with Color 3, work rem with Color 1; on ndl 2, work first and second sts with Color 1, work rem with Color 2; on ndl 3, work first and second sts with Color 2, work rem with Color 3.

Continue in this manner until the hat measures 7 (10½, 13)". Begin points as described in the main pattern.

Variation: Fair Isle Jester Hat
Materials
1 skein, (Color 1)
1 skein, (Color 2)
1 skein, (Color 3)

Directions
Work jester hat as described in the main pattern, using Color 1 for the rolled brim and Color 2 for ribbing. Work charts below with Colors 1 and 3. Work each point in a different color.

Reversible Scarves

design by Elizabeth Wellenstein

Finished size
6½ wide, and as long as you like
Gauge
Approx 5 sts = 1"
Gauge is not critical for this pattern

Materials
1 skein #8401 (Grey; C1)
1 skein #7807 (Regal; C2)
US 7 (4.5 mm) circ ndl

Directions
Note: At the end of each row you will see either the word *turn* or *slide*. *Turn* means simply to turn your work; *slide* means slide your work to the opposite end of the ndl.

CO 30 sts withC2 and slide them to the opposite end of your ndl. Work the following 4 rows to desired length:

Row 1: attach C1 and knit across; turn
Row 2: knit with C2; slide
Row 3: purl with C1; turn
Row 4: purl with C2; slide
Rep rows 1-4 to desired length.

Variation: Textured Stripes
Materials
1 skein # 8401 (Grey; C1)
1 skein # 9404 (Ruby; C2)

Directions
CO 31 sts with C1; slide. Work the following 4 rows to desired length:
Row 1: attach C2, k1, * p1, k1; rep from *; turn
Row 2: rep Row 1 with C2; slide
Rows 3 and 4: rep rows 1 and 2 with C1

Variation: Ribbed Stripes
Materials
1 skein # 9429 (Mossy Rock; C1)
1 skein # 8234 (Pistachio; C2)

Directions
CO 31 sts with C1; slide. Work the following 4 rows to desired length:

Row 1: attach C2, k1, *p1, k1; rep from *; turn
Row 2: with C2, p1, *k1, p1; rep from *; slide
Row 3: rep row 2 with C1; turn
Row 4: rep row 1 with C1; slide

Variation: Textured Check Scarf
Materials
1 skein # 2414 (Ginger; C1)
1 skein # 7807 (Regal; C2)

Directions
CO 31 sts with C2; slide. Work the following 4 rows to desired length:

Row 1: attach C1, k1, *sl 1 wyif, k1; rep from *; turn
Row 2: with C1, p1, *k1, p1; rep from *; slide
Rows 3 and 4: rep Rows 1 and 2 with C2

Variation: Ribbed Lattice Scarf
Materials
1 skein # 8234 (Pistachio; C1)
1 skein # 7807 (Regal; C2)

Directions
CO 29 sts with C2; slide. Work the following 4 rows to desired length:

Row 1: attach C1, k1, *p1, sl 1 wyib, p1, k1; rep from *; turn
Row 2: with C1, p1, *k1, sl 1 wyif, k1, p1; rep from *; slide
Row 3: with C2, p1, *k1, p1; rep from *; turn
Row 4: with C2, k1, *p1, k1; rep from *; slide

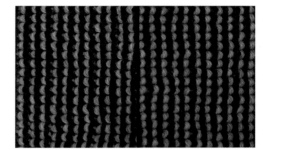

Pattern 56

Pattern 57

Pattern 58

Pattern 59

Pattern 60

Lace Headbands

design by Elizabeth Wellenstein

Harlequin Lace Headband
Finished sizes
Women's S/M (L) 20 (21½)" circumference

Gauge
6 sts = 1" worked in st st on size 4 ndl in the rnd

Materials
1 skein #9419 (Vermeer Blue)
US 4 (3.5 mm) 16" circ ndl
US 6 (4.25 mm) 16" circ ndl

Harlequin Lace
Rnd 1: *yo, k2tog tbl, k6; rep from *
Rnd 2 and all even rnds: knit
Rnd 3: *k1, yo, k2tog tbl, k3, k2tog, yo; rep from *
Rnd 5: *k2, yo, k2tog tbl, k1, k2tog, yo, k1; rep from *
Rnd 7: *k1, yo, k2tog, yo, k3tog, yo, k2tog tbl, yo; rep from *
Rnd 9: *k4, yo, k2tog tbl, k2; rep from *
Rnd 11: *k2, k2tog, yo, k1, yo, k2tog tbl, k1; rep from *
Rnd 13: *k1, k2tog, yo, k3, yo, k2tog tbl; rep from *
Rnd 15: *k2tog, yo, k2tog tbl, yo, k1, yo, k2tog, yo; rep from *
Rnd 16: knit

Pattern 61

Directions
CO 120 (128) sts with smaller ndl for the inner layer of the headband. Pm and join ends, being careful not to twist the first rnd. Work in st st until band measures 2½" from cast-on edge. Purl 1 rnd. Change to larger ndl for the outer band. Work Rows 1-16 of Harlequin Lace pattern.

Join inner and outer layers
Fold work at purl ridge. The cast-on edge will meet the row of live sts on your ndl and they will be joined with applied I-Cord. Work applied I-cord as follows: with RS (outer band) facing you, pick up first edge st from the inner band and place it on the LHN next to the first st of the outer band. Be sure to pick up your sts consistently! CO 3 sts on the RHN. Transfer them to the LHN. K2, sl 1, k2tog tbl, psso. *Pick up next edge st from inner band and place it on the LHN. Replace 3 sts from RHN to LHN. K2, slip 1, k2tog tbl, psso. Repeat from *. When all sts have been worked, break yarn leaving an 8" tail. Thread tapestry ndl with tail and pull strand through 3 rem sts. Then thread ndl through the opposite end of I-cord to close up any gap. Secure and weave in end.

Now a rnd of I-cord is applied to the purl ridge. Although this edge is best worked with 2 dpns in the same size as you knit the outer band, it can also be worked with a circ ndl. With RS facing, CO 3 sts to RHN. With same ndl, pick up first st of purl ridge and slide all 4 sts to opposite end of ndl. Transfer ndl to left hand. K2, sl 1, k1 tbl, psso. * Pick up next st and slide all 4 sts to opposite end of ndl. K2, slip 1, k1 tbl, psso. Repeat from * until all sts have been worked. Break yarn leaving a 6" tail. Secure and weave in end.

Variation: Diamond Eyelet Headband
Finished Sizes 20 (21½)"
Materials
1 skein #8415 (Cranberry)

Diamond Eyelet Lace
Rnd 1: * k4, yo, k2tog tbl, k1; rep from *
Rnd 2 and all even rows: knit
Rnd 3: *k3, yo, k2tog tbl, yo, k2tog tbl; rep from *
Rnd 5: rep rnd 1
Rnd 7: *k1, yo, k2tog tbl, k4; rep from *
Rnd 9: *yo, k2tog tbl, yo, k2tog tbl, k3; rep from *
Rnd 11: rep rnd 7
Rnds 13-18: rep rnds 1-6

Directions
CO 119 (126) sts with smaller ndl. Work as described in the main pattern, substituting Diamond Eyelet Lace for Harlequin Lace. Finish as described in the main pattern.

Variation: Zig-Zag Lace Headband
Finished Sizes 20 (21½)"
Materials
1 skein #9456 (Sapphire Heather)

Zig-Zag Lace
Rnd 1: knit
Rnd 2 and all even rnds: knit
Rnd 3: *k8, k2tog, yo; rep from *
Rnd 5: *yo, k2tog tbl, k5, k2tog, yo, k1; rep from *
Rnd 7: *k1, yo, k2tog tbl, k3, (k2tog, yo) twice; rep from *
Rnd 9: *(yo, k2tog tbl) twice , k1, (k2tog, yo) twice, k1; rep from *
Rnd 11: *k1, yo, k2tog tbl, yo, k3tog, yo, k2tog, yo, k2; rep from *
Rnd 13: *k2, yo, k2tog tbl, yo, k3 tog, yo, k3; rep from *
Rnd 15: *k3, yo, k3tog, yo, k4; rep from *
Rnd 17: knit

Directions
CO 120 (130) sts with smaller ndl. Work as described in the main pattern, substituting Zig-Zag Lace for Harlequin Lace. Finish as described in the main pattern.

Variation: Heart Lace Headband
Finished sizes 19½ (21½)" circumference
Materials
1 skein #9451 (Lake Chelan Heather)

Heart Lace
Rnd 1: *k6, yo, k2tog tbl, k5; rep from *
Rnd 2 and all even rnds: knit
Rnd 3: * k4, k2tog, yo, k1, yo, k2tog tbl, k4; rep from *
Rnd 5: *k3, k2tog, yo, k3 yo, k2tog tbl, k3; rep from *
Rnd 7: *k2, k2tog, yo, k5, yo, k2tog tbl, k2; rep from *
Rnd 9: *k1, k2tog, yo, k7, yo, k2tog tbl, k1; rep from *
Rnd 11: *k2tog, yo, k4, yo , k2tog tbl, k3, yo, k2tog tbl; rep from *
Rnd 13: *k1, yo, k2tog tbl, k1, k2tog, yo, k1, yo, k2tog tbl, k1, k2tog, yo, k1; rep from *
Rnd 15: * k2, yo, k3tog, yo, k3, yo, k3tog, yo, k2; rep from *
Rnd 16: knit

Directions
CO 117 (130) sts with smaller ndl. Work as described in the main pattern, substituting Heart Lace for Harlequin Lace. Finish as described in the main pattern.

Variation: Spiral Eyelet Headband
Finished Sizes 20 (21½)"
Materials
1 skein #9451 (Lake Chelan Heather)

Spiral Eyelet
Rnd1: *yo, k2tog tbl, k2; rep from *
Rnd 2: *k1, yo, k2tog tbl, k1; rep from *
Rnd 3: *k2, yo, k2tog tbl; rep from *
Rnd 4: *k2tog tbl, k2, yo; rep from *
Repeat rnds 1-4 until panels match

Directions
CO 120 (128) sts with smaller ndl. Work as described in the main pattern, substituting Spiral Eyelet for Harlequin Lace. Finish as described in the main pattern.

Mittens

design by Elizabeth Wellenstein

Finished Sizes
Childs L/Adult S, (M, L, XL) 7½ (8, 8½, 9½)" circumference

Gauge
6 sts = 1" worked in st st on larger ndl in the rnd

Materials
1 skein #9457 (Cobalt Heather)
Set of US 3 (3.25 mm) dpns
Set of US 5 (3.75) dpns or size to obtain gauge.

Directions
Cuff
CO 36 (40, 44, 48) sts with smaller dpn. You will have 9 (10, 11, 12) sts on each ndl. Join ends, being careful not to twist the circle. Pm between first and second st. Work k2, p2 ribbing for 2½ (2¾, 3, 3)" or to desired length. Change to larger ndls. Knit 1 rnd, then begin increase rnds as follows: inc 4 sts evenly in next rnd to 40 (44, 48, 52) sts, knit 1 rnd, inc 4 sts evenly in next rnd to 44 (48, 52, 56) sts. Knit 1¾ (2¼, 2¼, 2½)" from top of ribbing or until you reach base of the thumb.

Thumb placement
For right thumb, knit 9 (9, 10, 11) sts with a piece of waste yarn. Slip waste yarn sts back to LHN and knit again with working yarn. Finish rnd. For left thumb placement, knit 13 (15, 16, 17) sts. Knit next 9 (9, 10, 11) sts with a piece of waste yarn. Slip waste yarn sts back to LHN and knit again with working yarn. Finish rnd.

Mitten
Continue in st st until piece measures 3¾ (4¼, 4¾, 5)" from waste yarn or about 1½ (1¾, 2, 2)" from desired length. Dec for top as follows:
Rnd 1: * k9 (10, 11, 12), k2tog; rep from * (40, 44, 48, 52 sts)
Rnd 2: knit
Rnd 3: * k8 (9, 10, 11), k2tog, rep from * (36, 40, 44, 48 sts)
Rnd 4: knit
Now dec every rnd, following the above pattern, until 8 sts rem. Cut yarn, leaving a 12" tail. Draw tail through rem sts tightly to close up top. Thread yarn to inside and secure.

Pattern 68 and 69

Thumb finishing
Pick out waste yarn at thumb and place live sts on 2 dpns. Redistribute 17 (17, 19, 21) live sts evenly on 3 dpns by working one rnd and, at the same time, pick up and knit into the back of 1 st at each corner to close up gaps (19,19, 21, 23 sts). Work until thumb measures 2 (2¼, 2½, 2½)" or ¼" less than desired length. K2tog around for 2 rnds or until 8 or fewer sts remain. Cut yarn, leaving a 12" tail. Draw tail through rem sts tightly. Thread yarn to inside and secure.

Variation: Two-Color Mittens
Materials
1 skein # 9457 (Cobalt Heather)
1 skein #9444 (Tangerine Heather)

Directions
Work mittens through thumb placement as described in the main pattern. Follow Chart A to work mitten body until dec rnds begin. Work dec rnds and thumb in a single color.

Variation: Bright Checkered Mittens
Materials
1 skein #8885 (Purple)
1 skein #7814 (Chartreuse)

Directions
Work mittens through thumb placement as described in the main pattern. Follow Chart B to work mitten body until dec rnds begin. You can work the dec rnds in a single color as described in the main pattern, or you can follow Chart C for a lice color pattern. The thumb can also be worked in the lice pattern.

Variation: Mitten with Ruffled Edge
Materials
1 skein #8885 (Purple)

Directions
With smaller dpns, CO 108 (120, 132, 144) sts. Join ends, being careful not to twist the circle. Pm between first and second st to secure. Work ruffle as follows: knit until ruffle is 2" long , or to desired length, then k2tog around. Knit one rnd even, then *k1, k2tog one rnd. Work k2, p2 ribbing for 1". Continue with directions for the mitten of your choice, beginning after the ribbing rnds.

Variation: Mitten with Scrunch Edge
Materials
1 skein #9444 (Tangerine Heather)

Directions
CO 36 (40, 44, 48) sts with smaller dpns. Join ends, being careful not to twist sts, and pm between first and second st to secure. Work alternating pattern of 4 rnds rev st st and 3 rnds st st. Cont until cuff is desired length. Work mitten as described in the main pattern or any of the variations.

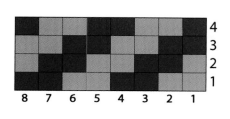

Chart A

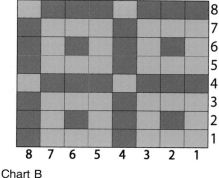

Chart B

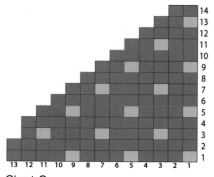

Chart C

Garter Stitch Headbands

design by Mary Lou Egan

Finished sizes

XS (4-6 yrs), S (6-12 yrs), M (12 yrs-adult), L (adult)

This earwarmer is knit lengthwise, so you can decide how wide you want the band to be by the number of stitches you cast on, and how long by the length of band you knit.

Gauge

3.5-4 sts = 1"

Gauge is not critical because the size is mainly determined by the length.

Materials

1 skein, #9435 (Quatro) , worked double (using two strands)

US 9 (5.5 mm), 10 (6.0 mm) or 10.5 (6.5 mm) ndls

Garter Stitch with I-Cord Edging

Row 1: Knit to the last three sts, yf, sl 3 sts purlwise
Rep row 1.

Twisted Rib

Row 1: k3, *k1 tbl, p1 tbl; rep from *, end sl 3 purlwise

Row 2: k3, *p1 tbl, k1 tbl; rep from *, end sl 3 purlwise

Directions

With two strands held together, CO 14 (14, 16, 16) sts using a provisional cast-on method. Work in Garter Stitch with I-Cord until piece measures 5½ (5¾, 6, 6½)".

Work forehead shaping as follows:

Row 1: k3, k2tog, work to 5 sts before edge, k2tog, sl 3 purlwise.

Pattern 71

Row 2: knit to last 3 sts, sl 3 purlwise. Rep Rows 1-2 once.

Work Twisted Rib for 5 (5½, 6, 6)", then inc as follows:

Row 1: k3, m1, knit to last 3 sts, m1, sl 3 purlwise.

Row 2: Knit to last 3 sts, sl 3 purlwise. Repeat row 1 once more.

Work again in Garter Stitch with I-Cord for 5½ (5¾, 6, 6½)" or to desired length.

To finish, join ends using 3-needle bind-off or graft edges together.

Variation: Garter Stitch Headband with Contrast Edge

Materials

1/2 skein #8555 (Black; Color A)
1/2 skein #9435 (Quattro; Color B)

Directions

Use strands of two different color yarns, Color A for the I-cord edge and Color B for the center. Work the pattern stitch using Color A for the I-cord edge sts and work both tog for the center of the band. *Every 4 or 5 rows, do an extra row in the*

Pattern 72

I-cord edge on the knit side to avoid it being tighter than the middle sts. Work as described in the main pattern until the forehead shaping.

Work forehead shaping as follows:

Row 1: k3, k2tog, knit to last 3 sts, sl 3 purlwise

Row 2: Knit to last 3 sts, sl 3 purlwise
Repeat these two rows one more time, then work even in garter stitch with I-cord for 5 (5½, 6, 6)".

Work increases:

Row 1: k3, m1, knit to last 3 sts, sl 3 purlwise
Row 2: Knit to last 3 sts, sl 3 purlwise
Repeat Row 1.

Continue working in Garter Stitch with I-cord Edge for 5½ (5¾, 6, 6½)" or desired length.

To finish, join ends using 3-needle bind-off.

Fisherman Scarf

design by Patti Pierce Stone

Finished size
About 6" x 46"

Gauge
10 sts x 12 rows = 2" in st st

Materials
1 skein #7810 (Amethyst)
US 7 (4.5 mm) ndl

Note: These patterns have 2-st I-cord edges: the first two sts in each row are knit, the last 2 sts of each row are slipped purlwise, with the yarn forward.

Border Pattern
Row 1 (RS): k2, *k1, p1; rep from * to last 2 sts, sl 2 wyif
Row 2: k2, *p1, k1; rep from * to last 2 sts, sl 2 wyif
Row 3: k2, *p1, k1; rep from * to last 2 sts, sl 2 wyif
Row 4: k2, *k1, p1; rep from * to last 2 sts, sl 2 wyif
Row 5: k2, *k1, p1; rep from * to last 2 sts, sl 2 wyif
Row 6: k2, *p1, k1; rep from * to last 2 sts, sl 2 wyif
Row 7: k2, *k1, p1; rep from * to last 2 sts, sl 2 wyif

Faux Cable 1
Row 1 (and all WS rows): k3, p7, k1, p11, k1, p7, k1, sl 2 wyif
Row 2: k2, p1, yo, k2, ssk, k3, p1, k11, p1, k3, k2tog, k2, yo, p1, sl 2 wyif
Row 4: k2, p1, k1, yo, k2, ssk, k2, p1, k11, p1, k2, k2tog, k2, yo, k1, p1, sl 2 wyif
Row 6: k2, p1, k2, yo, k2, ssk, k1, p1, k11, p1, k1, k2tog, k2, yo, k2, p1, sl2 wyif
Row 8: k2, p1, k3, yo, k2, ssk, p1, k11, p1, k2tog, k2, yo, k3, p1, sl 2 wyif

Ribbing
Row 1: k2, *p1, k1; rep from * to last 2 sts, sl 2 wyif
Row 2 (WS): k2, *k1, p1; rep from * to last 2 sts, sl 2 wyif

Faux Cable 2
Row 1 (and all WS rows): k3, p7, k1, p11, k1, p7, k1, sl 2 wyif
Row 2: k2, p1, k3, k2tog, k2, yo, p1, k11, p1, yo, k2, ssk, k3, p1, sl 2 wyif
Row 4: k2, p1, k2, k2tog, k2, yo, k1, p1, k11, p1, k1, yo, k2, ssk, k2, p1, sl 2 wyif
Row 6: k2, p1, k1, k2tog, k2, yo, k2, p1, k11, p1, k2, yo, k2, ssk, k1, p1, sl 2 wyif

Pattern 73

Row 8: k2, p1, k2tog, k2, yo, k3, p1, k11, p1, k3, yo, k2, ssk, p1, sl 2 wyif

Directions
CO 33 sts using a long-tail cast-on method. Work rows 1-7 of Border Pattern. Work rows 1-8 of Faux Cable 1 10 times, ending with a WS row. Work Rib for 17", ending with a RS row. Work row 1-8 of Faux Cable 2 10 times, ending with a WS row. Work 7 rows of Border Pattern, working backwards from row 7 to row 1. Bind off with a sewn cast-off to match cast-on.

Variation: Fisherman's Scarf in Stockinette Stitch
Materials
1 skein #8400 (Charcoal Grey)

Stockinette with I-Cord
Row 1 (WS): k2, purl to last 2 sts, sl 2 wyif

Row 2 (RS): k2, k28 (*or insert any stitch multiple of 4 here*), sl 2 wyif

Directions
CO 33 sts. Work rows 1-7 of Border Pattern. On next row, k2, k13, k2tog, k14, sl 2 wyif (32 st).
Work in Stockinette and I-Cord pattern until scarf measures 13" from border. End with a WS row. On the next row, k2, k14, m1, k14, sl 2 wyif (33 st).

Work Ribbing for 17", beginning on row 2 (WS) and ending on a WS row. On the next row, k2, k13, k2tog, k14, sl 2 wyif (32 st). Work in Stockinette and I-Cord pattern for 13", ending on the WS and increasing one st on the last row (33 st). Work 7 rows of Border Pattern, working backwards from row 7 to row 1. Bind off with a sewn cast-off to match cast-on.

32

Hats Off!

design by Elizabeth Wellenstein

Match a handband with your choice of top for endless possibilities.

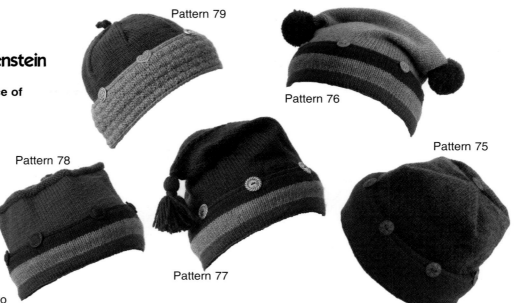

Pattern 79

Pattern 76

Pattern 78

Pattern 75

Pattern 77

Solid Color Headband
Finished Sizes
Child age 5 to adult S (adult M/L)
21½ (23 ¼)" circumference

Gauge
5.5 sts x 7.5 rows = 1" worked in st st on larger ndl in the rnd

Materials
1 skein #8885 (Dark Plum)
US 4 (3.5 mm) 16" (40 cm) circ ndl
US 6 (4.25 mm) 16" circ ndl, or size to obtain gauge

Directions
CO 119 (128) sts with smaller ndl for the inner layer of the headband. Pm and join ends, being careful not to twist the circle. Work in st st until band measures 2½" from cast-on edge. Purl 1 rnd. Change to larger ndl for the outer band and continue in st st until band measures 2½" from purl ridge.

Fold at purl ridge. The cast-on edge will meet the round of live sts on your needle and they will be joined with a Finishing I-cord. Work Finishing I-cord. Work a rnd of Invisible I-cord buttonholes. You should have 7(8) evenly spaced, hidden buttonholes around the top of your headband (there will be an extra st at the end if you are knitting the smaller size, but this is not noticeable).

Note: You are not limited to solid colors! Try stripes in your bands for creative color combinations with your hats.

Variation: Basketweave Headband
Materials
1 skein #4011 (Sparrow)

Basketweave Pattern
Rnd 1 and 2: knit
Rnd 3 and 4: *p2, k2, rep from *
Rnd 5 and 6: knit
Rnd 7 and 8: *k2, p2, rep from *

Directions
CO 120 (128) sts with smaller ndl for the inner layer of the headband. Pm and join ends, being careful not to twist the circle. Work in st st until band measures 2¾" from cast-on edge. Purl 1 rnd. Change to larger ndl for the outer band and work basketweave pattern until a total of 22 rows are completed, ending with 2 knit rnds. Fold at purl ridge and finish as described for the solid color headband.

Note: You can use other stitch patterns for your headband…just work in multiples of 4.

Button Top
Finished sizes
Child age 5 to adult S (adult M/L)
21¾ (23¼)" circumference

Gauge
5.5 sts x 7.5 rows = 1" worked in st st on larger ndl in the rnd

Materials
1 skein #9459 (Midnight Heather)
8 (9) ¾ to 7/8" diameter buttons
US 4 (3.5 m) 16" (40 cm) circ ndl
US 6 (4.25 mm) 16" circ ndl, or size to obtain gauge
2 extra needles for 3-needle bind-off

Directions
CO 120 (128) sts with smaller ndl. Pm and join ends, being careful not to twist the circle. Work in k3, p1 ribbing for 7 rnds. Change to larger ndl. Work in st st until piece measures 7 (7½)" from cast-on edge. Turn piece inside out. Transfer ½ of sts to another ndl and work 3-needle bind-off to end. Cut a 10" tail. Turn hat right side out and push out the corners created by the bind-off. Thread tail through tapestry needle and push it out through the corner. Then secure other corner with another stitch and add the button, centering it on top of the hat.

Make a stitch in the top of the hat to secure the corners and button there.

Attach Buttons
Begin with the button you would like to place at the center back and determine which st that will be on the hat. With yarn and darning needle, sew buttons in place so that the bottom edge of the button is sitting right above the top row of ribbing, so that no gap between the two pieces will show. Sew 7 buttons every 17 sts for the smaller size, and 8 buttons every 16 sts for the larger size. Or you can lay the hat top flat and smooth and pin it to the band to match up with the buttonholes. You may need to adjust your pinning as you work around the band. Button the top to band.

Variation: Jester Top
Materials
1 skein #4010 (Straw)
7 (8) ¾ to 7/8" buttons

Directions
Work Button Top as described above, but do not attach corners to center of hat. Instead, work a 3-needle bind off, weave in ends, and then add pom-poms to each tip.

Variation: Stocking Cap
Finished sizes
S (M/L) 21¾ (23¼)" circumference

Materials
1 skein #7808 (Purple Hyacinth)
7 (8) ¾ to 7/8" buttons

33

Double dec (dd) = slip next 2 sts knitwise together onto right ndl, k third st, pass 2 sl sts over knit st.

Directions
CO 120 (128) with smaller ndl. Pm and join ends, being careful not to twist the circle. Work k3, p1 ribbing for 7 rnds. Change to larger ndl, and work in st st for 6 (7)" from cast-on edge. Begin decreasing as follows (switching to dpns when sts no longer fit comfortably around the circ ndl):

Rnd 1: * k27 (29), dd, rep from *
Rnd 2 and 3: knit
Rnd 4: k26 (28), dd, *k25 (27), dd, rep from *
Rnd 5 and 6: knit
Rnd 7: k24 (26), dd, * k23 (25), dd, rep from *
Rnd 8 and 9: knit.
Rnd 10: k22 (24), dd, * k21 (23), dd, rep from *
Rnd 11 and 12: knit.
Rnd 13: k20 (22), dd, * k19 (21), dd, rep from *
Rnd 14 and 15: knit

Continue decreasing until 4 sts rem. Cut 6" tail, thread through tapestry needle, pull yarn through 4 sts and secure on the inside of hat. Attach buttons as described for the Button Top. Make a tassle and attach to top.

Variation: Flat Top
Finished sizes
S (M/L) 21¾ (23 ¼)" circumference

Materials
1 skein #2414 (Ginger)
7 (8) ¾" to ⅞" buttons

Directions
CO 120 (130) with smaller ndl. Pm and join ends, being careful not to twist the circle. Work k4, p1 ribbing for 7 rnds. Change to larger ndl. Work in st st for 4 (4½)" from cast-on edge. Work purl rows as follows:
for smaller size, p2tog, purl 5 rnds, then knit 2 rnds (119 sts). For the larger size, purl 5 rnds, inc 3, then knit 2 rnds (133 sts). Begin decreasing as follows (switching to dpns when sts no longer fit comfortably around the circ ndl):

Rnd 1: * k14 (16), dd, rep from *
Rnd 2: knit
Rnd 3: knit around (k15, dd, *k14, dd, rep from *)

Rnd 4: k13, dd, *k12, dd, rep from * (knit around)
Rnd 5: knit around (k13, dd, *k12, dd, rep from *)
Rnd 6: k11, dd, *k10, dd, rep from * (knit around)
Rnd 7: knit around (k11, dd, *k10, dd, rep from *)
Rnd 8: knit
Rnd 9: k9, dd, *k8, dd, rep from *
Rnd 10: knit
Rnd 11: k7, dd, *k6, dd, rep from *
Rnd 12: knit
Rnd 13: knit around (k5, dd, *k4, dd, rep from *)
Rnd 14: k5, dd, *k4, dd, rep form * (knit around)
Rnd 15: knit around (k3, dd, *k2, dd, rep from *)
Rnd 16: k3, dd, *k2, dd, rep from * to end of rnd (knit around)
Rnd 17: knit (k1, dd, *dd, rep from *; 7 sts rem)
Rnd 18: knit (k2tog until 4 sts rem)
For Size S:
Rnd 19: k1, dd, *dd, rep, from *; 7 sts rem
Rnd 20: k2tog until 4 sts rem

Work I-cord for 2" as follows: *k4 onto a dpn. Slide sts to opposite end of ndl and transfer it to your left hand. Break yarn, leaving a 6" strand for finishing. With tapestry needle and strand, draw the 4 I-cord loops tog and pull the strand down through the center of cord. Tack down at the base on the inside of the hat. Tie a knot at the base of the cord.

Piping
Thread a tapestry needle with about 40" of yarn. Turn hat inside out and find the st st strip that runs around the top of your hat. You will be creating a thin tube by bringing the top and bottom edges together. Whipstitch the tube closed by picking up the top and bottom purl bumps alternately around the circumference of the hat. Be sure to pick up each st so that the tube holds it's shape well. This will create the piping around the top of the hat. Attach buttons as described in the Button Top pattern.

Variation: Dome Top
Finished sizes
S (M/L) 21¾ (23¼)" circumference

Materials
1 skein #9429 (Mossy Rock)
7 (8), ¾" to ⅞" buttons

Directions
CO 120 (128) with smaller ndl. Pm and join ends, being careful not to twist the

circle. Work k3, p1 ribbing for 7 rnds. Change to larger ndl, dec 1 (2) sts evenly in next rnd to 119 (126) sts. Work in st st for 3 ½ (4)" from cast-on edge. Begin decreasing as follows (switching to dpns when sts no longer fit comfortably around the circ ndl):

Rnd 1: * k15 (16), k2tog, rep from *
Rnd 2 and every even rnd: knit
Rnd 3: *k14 (15), k2tog, rep from *
Rnd 5: *k13 (14), k2tog, rep from *
Rnd 7: *k12 (13), k2tog, rep from *

Continue dec until there are 4 sts between dec. Dec every round until 7 sts rem. K2tog until 4 sts rem. Knit I-cord for 2" as described in the Flap Top pattern. Attach buttons as described in the Button Top pattern.

Work a Finishing I-cord as follows:
With RS (outer band) facing you pick up first edge st from the inner band (the side worked with the smaller needles), inserting the needle from front to back, place it on the LHN next to the first st of the outer band. Be sure to pick up your sts consistently!

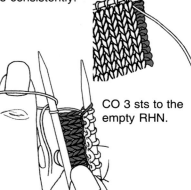

CO 3 sts to the empty RHN.

Move the CO stitches to LHN. The live end of the yarn will be at the third stitch from the tip of the needle.

K2, slip 1,

k2tog tbl,   psso.

*Pick up next edge st from inner band with the RHN.

Move the 4 sts currently on the RHN to LHN. K2, slip 1, k2tog tbl, psso as before. Repeat from *.

When all edge sts have been worked, there will be 3 stitches remaining on the RHN. Break the yarn leaving an 8" tail.

Thread the tail through a tapestry needle and pull it through the loops of the 3 remaining sts.

To join the end of the I-cord to the beginning, insert the needle through the starting stitches of the I-cord to close any gap. Secure with a couple of stitches and weave in the end.

Work a round of Invisible I-Cord buttonholes as follows:
(attached to purl ridge on fold of band)

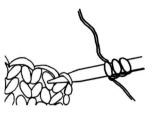

You may prefer to work this edge with 2 DPNs in the larger size used to knit the outer band. It can also be worked with circular needles.

With RS facing you and using yarn the same color as the edge to which it is being applied, CO 3 sts to RHN.

With the tip of the RHN, pick up first st of purl ridge by inserting the needle from back to front. Be sure to pick up your sts consistently!

Take the needle in your left hand and slide stitches toward the tip. K2, slip 1, k1 tbl, psso. (This is similar to steps of the Finishing I-cord.)

*With the tip of the RHN, pick up next st from purl ridge and slide all 4 sts to opposite end of needle. K2, slip 1, k1 tbl, psso. Repeat from * until a total of 14(13) I-cord rows have been attached to the folded edge.

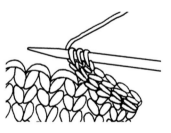

Create a buttonhole. K 2(2) unattached I-cord rows without picking up the next edge stitch. Just slide the 3 sts to the opposite end of the needle and knit across.

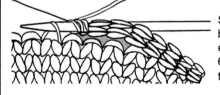

Skip 3(3) edge sts and then attach the I-cord as before. Repeat these steps until there are 3 edge sts remaining unworked. You should have 6(7) evenly spaced hidden buttonholes around the top of your headband.

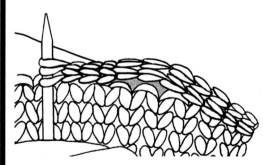

To finish, work 2 unattached I-cord rows as before. Break the yarn leaving a 6" tail. Thread the tail through a tapestry needle and pull it through the loops of the 3 remaining sts. Skipping the 3 unworked edge stitches, insert the needle through the starting stitches of the I-cord to close any gap and create the last buttonhole. (7(8) total buttonholes). Secure with a couple of stitches and weave in the end.

Cropped Sweaters

design by Urban Tribal Wear Designs

Finished Sizes
Chest size 33 (39, 42, 48)"

Gauge
5.5 sts x 7rows = 1" worked in st st with larger ndl

Materials
5 (6, 6, 7) skeins #7803 (Magenta; MC)
1 (2) skeins #8909 (Raspberry; CC)
US 7 (4.5 mm) ndl
US 6 (4.0 mm) 16" or 24" circ ndl for neck finishing

C4F (Cable 4 Front): slip 2 sts onto cable needle, knit next 2 sts, knit 2 from cable needle

Directions

Back

With smaller needle and CC, CO 92 (108, 116, 132) sts. Work in k4, p4 ribbing for 2½". Change to larger ndl and work one cable row as follows: *c4f, p4, repeat from * to end of row. Next, [work 3 rows in rib pattern and one row in cable pattern], 2 times. Work 3 rows in rib pattern. Change to MC and work in st st until the piece measures 12 (12½, 13, 13½)".

Begin armhole shaping

Bind off 5 (8, 9, 11) sts at beg of next 2 rows. Dec 1 st each side every RS row 4 (7, 8, 11) times. Continue in st st until the piece measures 7½ (8, 8½, 9)" from armhole bind-off.

Shape shoulders and back neck

Bind off 7 (7, 8, 8) sts at beg of next row. At beg of next row bind off 7 (7, 8, 8) sts, work 13 (14, 15, 16) sts, attach a second ball of yarn and bind off 34 (34, 36, 40) back neck sts. Complete row. At beg of next row, bind off 6 (7, 7, 8) sts and dec 1 st at each neck edge. Bind off 6 (7, 7, 8) sts at beg of next row. Bind off 6 (7, 7, 7) sts at beg of next 2 rows. Cast off.

Front

Work as for back including all shaping, and *at the same time*, when piece measures 19 (20, 21, 21½)", work neck shaping as follows: work to center 24 (24, 26, 26) sts, attach another ball of yarn, bind off center 24 (24, 26, 26) sts, complete row. Work both sides at once. Dec 1 st at each neck edge every RS row 6 (6, 6, 8) times.
Work until piece measures 7½ (8, 8½, 9)" from armhole bind-off. Shape shoulders to correspond with back.

Pattern 82

Full sleeves

With smaller needles and CC, CO 46 (50, 52, 58) sts. Work in k4, p4 ribbing until the piece measures 3". Change to MC and larger ndl, and continue in st st. Work one RS row. Inc 1 st on each side every 4 rows 16 (16, 21, 16) times, then every 6 rows 5 (6, 3, 7) times. Continue even until piece measures 16½ (17½, 18, 18½)". Shape sleeve caps as follows: bind off 5 (8, 9, 11) sts at each side. Dec 1 st each side every RS row 0 (7, 8, 11) times, then every row 22 (17, 15, 11) times, then every RS row 0 (1, 2, 2) times. Bind off 3 (3, 4, 4) sts at beg of next 4 rows. Bind off remaining 14 (16, 16, 18) sts.

Finishing

Sew shoulders and seams. With smaller 16" circ ndl and CC, with RS facing, pick up 84 (88, 88, 104) sts evenly around the neck edge. Work in k1, p1 ribbing for 1". Bind off loosely in ribbing.

Variation: Turtleneck Cropped Sweater
Materials
5 (6, 6, 7) skeins #9429 (Mossy Rock; MC)
1 (2) skeins #8914 (Granny Smith; CC)

Directions
Work front, back, and sleeves as described in the main pattern. To finish, pick up 84 (88, 88, 104) neck sts, pm, join, and work in k2, p2 ribbing for 4". Change to larger ndl and continue in k2, p2 ribbing for an additional 4". Bind off very loosely in ribbing.

Variation: Cropped Sweater with ¾ Sleeve
Materials
5 (6, 6, 7) skeins #4001 (Smokey Blue)

Directions
Work front and back as described in the main pattern. Work sleeves as follows: with smaller ndl, CO 46 (50, 52, 58) sts. Work in k2, p2 ribbing for 2½". Change to larger ndl and continue in st st. Work one RS row. Inc 1 st on each side of every RS row 10 (10, 24, 9) times, then every 4 rows 11 (12, 0, 14) times. Continue until sleeve measures 12½ (13, 13½, 14)". Shape cap as described in the main pattern.

Variation: Cropped Sweater with V-Neck

Materials
5 (6, 6, 7) skeins #8686 (Brown; MC)
1 (2) skeins #9451 (Lake Chelan Heather; CC)

Directions
Work sweater back as described in the main pattern. Work front as described in the main pattern, until the piece measures 12½ (13½, 14, 14½)". Begin V-neck shaping as follows: work to center, attach another ball of yarn and complete row. Turn. Working both sides at once, dec 1 st at each neck edge every RS row 13 (10, 11, 13) times, then every 4 rows 4 (7, 7, 7) times. Continue until piece measures 7½ (8, 8½, 9)" from armhole bind off. Shape shoulders to correspond with back.

V-neck finishing
With smaller 16" circ ndl and RS facing, pick up 40 (40, 42, 46) sts from back neck, 39 (44, 46, 49) sts from left neck, pm, m1 in center, pick up 39 (44, 46, 49) sts from right neck. Pm for the end of rnd (119, 129, 135, 145 sts). Work in k1, p1 ribbing to within 2 sts of center marker, ssk, sl marker, k1, k2tog, work in k1, p1 ribbing to end of rnd. Rep this rnd for about 1". Bind off loosely in ribbing.

Variation: Textured Cropped Sweater

Materials
5 (6, 6, 7) skeins #9461 (Lime Heather)

Drop Stitch
Foundation Row (RS): k1, *p2, k1, yo, k1, p2, k2, rep from *, end p2, k1
Rows 1, 3, 5 (WS): p1, *k2, p2, k2, p3, rep from * end k2, p1
Rows 2, 4: k1, *p2, k3, p2, k2, rep from * end p2, k1
Row 6: k1, *p2, k1, drop next st off ndl and unravel down to the yo six rows below, k1, p2, k1, yo, k1, rep from *, end p2, k1
Rows 7, 9, 11: p1, *k2, p3, k2, p2, rep from *, end k2, p1
Rows 8, 10: k1, *p2, k2, p2, k3, rep from *, end p2, k1
Row 12: k1, *p2, k1, yo, k1, p2, k1, drop next st off needle and unravel six rows down as before, k1, rep from * end p2, k1

Directions
Work front and back as described in the main pattern, replacing ribbing and st st with Drop Stitch. Work sleeves in k2, p2 ribbing for entire sleeve.

Flat Handbags
design by Urban Tribal Wear Designs

Finished size
8" tall x 6" wide

Gauge
5.5 sts x 7 rows = 1" worked in st st

Materials
1 skein #8887 (Purple; Color 1)
1 skein #7802 (Pink; Color 2)
US 7 (4.5 mm) ndl

Directions
CO 34 sts with Color 1. Keeping the first and last st as a selvedge edge (slip these sts), work k1, p1 ribbing for 1" for the top of the bag. Work Chart A with both colors until the piece measures 16".

Make a textured flap by working Chart A as a knit/purl pattern in one color rather than two colors. When the flap is 7" long, bind off. Fold the bag and sew the sides. Make a 48" piece of 3-st I-cord and attach to each side of the bag.

Variation: Brocade Handbag
Materials
1 skein
1 button

Directions
CO 34 sts. Work in k1, p1 ribbing for 1". Work Rows 1-56 of Chart B for brocade pattern, then work 6 rows in st st for the bottom of the bag. Work Rows 56-1 of Chart B (reverse) for the back of the bag, so that the back and front will match when you fold the piece in half. Work k1, p1 ribbing for 1" and bind off.

Make a 4" piece of 3-st I-cord and sew it to the center back of the bag as a button loop. Sew on an appropriately-sized button. Make a 48" piece of 3-st I-cord for a handle. Sew to the top sides of the bag.

You can also work this brocade chart as a color pattern.

Variation: Honeycomb Cable Handbag
Finished Size 8" x 8"

Materials
1 skein
cn or dpn
Set of US 7 (4.5 mm) dpns

Pattern 85

Honeycomb Cable
Row 1 and all odd number rows (WS): purl
Row 2: *Sl 2 onto cn and hold in back, k2, k2 from cn, sl next 2 sts to cn and hold in front, k2, k2 from cn; rep from *
Row 4: knit

Row 6: *Sl 2 onto cn and hold in front, k2, k2 from cn, sl next 2 sts to cn and hold in back, k2, k2 from cn; rep from *
Row 8: knit

Directions
CO 34 sts. Keeping the first and last st as a selvedge edge, work 4 rows in k2, p2 ribbing, ending with a RS row. Work Honeycomb Cable until the piece measures 24". Work 4 rows in k2, p2 ribbing. Bind off in ribbing. Sew a bead and sequin into the center of each honeycomb (Diagram A).

Fold bag and sew sides (8" front, 8" back, 8" flap). Make a 48" piece of 3-st I-cord and attach to the sides of the bag for a handle.

Rebecca Bag
Materials
½ skein #9419 (Vermeer Blue; C1)
½ skein #8903 (Primaverra; C2)
½ skein #9469 (Hot Pink; C3)
½ skein #7825 (Orange Sherbet; C4)
½ skein #7809 (Violet; C5)
½ skein #8901 (Groseille; C6)

Seed Stitch
Row 1: *k1, p1; rep from *
Row 2: *p1, k1; rep from *

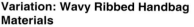

Directions
CO 32 sts with C6. Work 1½" in seed st. Work rows 1-46 of Chart C. Work 2" in st st in C1 for the bottom of the bag, then work rows 46-1 of Chart D (reverse) for the back of the bag, so that the back and front will match when you fold the piece in half. Switch to C6 and work seed st for 1½".

Fold the bag in half and sew sides. With dpns and RS facing, pick up and knit 30 sts across the front and 30 sts across the back. Pm, join, and work 4 rnds in st st. On next rnd, *k1, m1, rep from * to end of rnd. Knit 1 rnd. On next rnd *k1, m1, rep from * to end of rnd. Knit 1 rnd. Bind off loosely. Make a 48" long 3-st I-cord in orange and attach to the sides for a handle.

B (bobble): k in the front, back, and front of 1 st, turn, p3, turn, k3, turn, p3, turn, slip 1, k2tog, psso.

Chart B

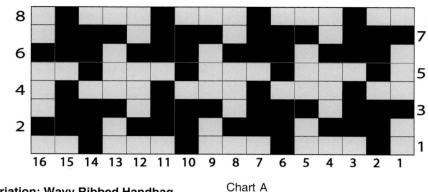

Chart A

Variation: Wavy Ribbed Handbag
Materials
1 skein

Directions
CO 34 sts. Keeping the first and last st as a selvedge edge, work 1" in seed st. Work Chart D until the piece measures 23". Work 1" in seed st. Fold bag so that an 8" flap remain. Sew sides. Make a 48" piece of 3-st I-cord and attach to the sides of the bag as a handle.

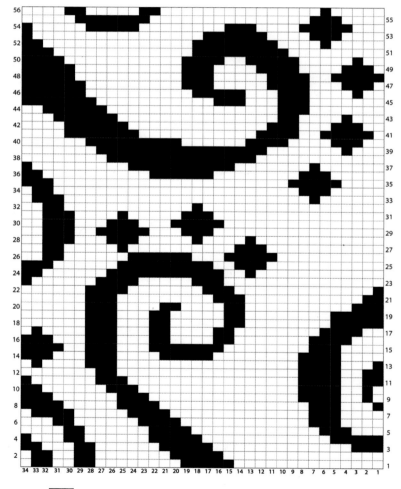

Diagram A

☐ purl on right side, knit on wrong side
■ knit on right side, purl on wrong side

38

Chart C

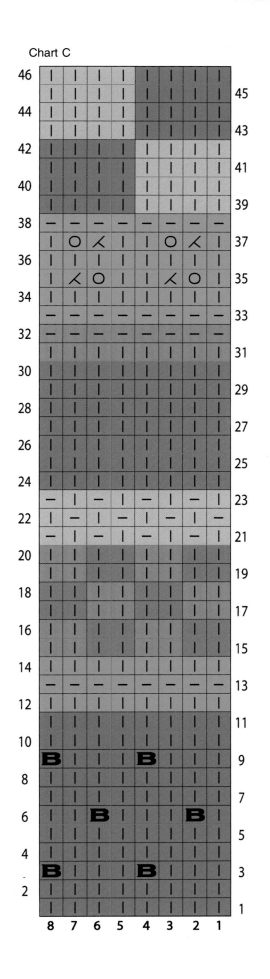

Chart D

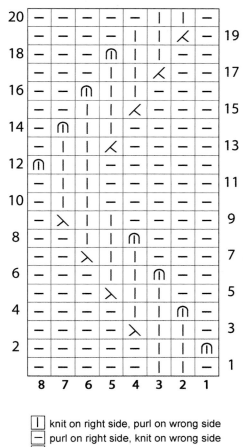

	knit on right side, purl on wrong side
−	purl on right side, knit on wrong side
⅄	k2tog
λ	ssk
m	increase - knit into the back of the stitch in the row below, then into the next stitch on the left needle

Doll Sweaters
design by Elizabeth Wellenstein

Finished Size
One size to fit 18" doll

Gauge
5 sts = 1"

Materials
Small amounts of #7802 (Cerise; C1), #7808 (Purple Hyacinth; C2), #7814 (Chartreuse; C3), and #9444 (Tangerine Heather; C4)
US 7 (4.5 mm) ndl

Directions
Front and Back
CO 35 sts with C3. Work rev st st for 3 rows. Change to C2 and, beginning with a purl row, work in st st until piece measures 6" from cast-on edge. Bind off. Work a second piece for the back.

Sleeve #1
CO 30 sts with C3. Work rev st st for 3 rows. Change to C4 and, beginning with a purl row, work in st st until piece measures 4" from cast-on edge. Bind off.

Sleeve #2
CO and work edging as for sleeve #1. Change to C1 and work same as sleeve #1.

Finishing
Sew 5 sts at one shoulder. Spread pieces out flat with RS facing. Count 5 sts in from outside edge and begin neck edging here. With C3, pick up and knit each st to within 5 sts of the other end. Turn, and beginning with a knit row (WS), work 3 rows in rev st st. Bind off in purl. Sew rem 5 shoulder sts and neck edge. Attach sleeves with an armhole depth of 3". Sew side seams and weave in ends.

Variation: Striped Doll Sweater
Materials
Small amounts of #7802 (Cerise; C1), #7814 (Chartreuse; C2), and #7808 (Purple Hyacinth; C3)

Directions
Work sweater as described in the main pattern, but work body and sleeve edges in rev st st with C1. Change to C3 and, beginning with a purl row, work in st st for 3 rows. Add C2 and continue in this pattern of 3 row stripes.

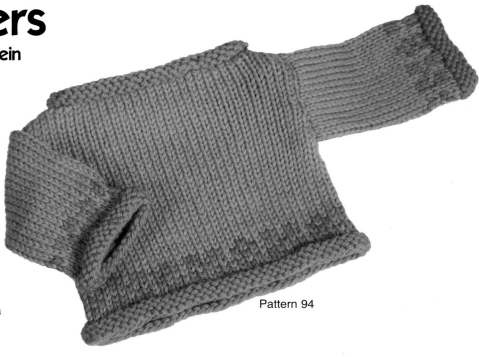
Pattern 94

Variation: Seeded Rib Stitch
Materials
Small amount of #7802 (Cerise; C1)
US 5 (3.75 mm) ndl
US 7 (4.5 mm) ndl, or size needed to obtain gauge.

Seeded Rib Stitch
Row 1 (RS): k2, * p1, k3, rep from * , end k2
Row 2 and every alt row: purl
Row 3: knit
Row 5: k4, *p1, k3, rep from *, end k4
Row 7: knit
Row 8: purl

Directions
Front and Back
CO 36 sts with smaller ndl. Work picot edge as follows: beginning with a purl row, work 3 rows in st st. On the next row (RS), *k2tog, yo, rep from *. Change to larger ndl and work 3 rows in st st. Continue in Seeded Rib Stitch until pieces measure 6" from bottom edge. Bind off. Work a second piece for the back.

Sleeves
With smaller ndl, CO 32 sts. Work picot edge as above. Then work in Seeded Rib Stitch until pieces measure 4" from bottom edge.

Finishing
Sew 5 sts at one shoulder. Spread pieces out flat with RS facing. Count 5 sts in from outside edge and begin neck edging

here. With larger ndl, knit up each st to within 5 sts of the other end. Turn and beginning with a purl row (WS), work 3 rows st st. On the next row (RS), *k2tog, yo, rep from *. Change to smaller ndl and work 3 rows in st st. Bind off. Sew the rem 5 shoulder sts and neck edge. Attach sleeves with an armhole depth of 3". Sew side seams and hem edges.

Variation: Snowflake Doll Sweater
Materials
Small amounts of #9438 (C1) and #7808 (Purple Hyacinth; C2)

Directions
Back
CO 35 sts with C2. Work rev st st for 3 rows. Change to C1 and, beginning with a purl row, work in st st until piece measures 6". Bind off.

Front
CO and work as for back until piece measures about 2½" from cast-on edge, ending with a WS row. On the next row, k9, pm, work Chart A, pm, k9. When chart is complete, continue in st st until piece is 6" from cast-on edge. Bind off.

Sleeves
CO 30 sts with C2. Work rev st st for 3 rows. Change to C1 and, beginning with a purl row, work in st st until piece measures 4" from cast on edge. Bind off.

Finish as described in the main pattern, using C2 for neck edging.

Variation: Fair Isle Doll Sweater
(knit in the round)
Materials
Small amounts of #7814(Chartreuse; C1) and #9444 (Tangerine Heather; C2)
US 7 (4.5 mm) 16" circ ndl, or size to obtain gauge
Set of US 7 dpns, or size to match circ ndl

Directions
CO 70 sts with C2. Pm and join ends, being careful not to twist the circle. Work in rev st st for 3 rnds. Add C1 and work Chart B. Continue in solid C1 until piece measures 3" from cast-on edge. Place 35 sts on a holder (front) and work rem 35 sts (back) flat in st st until piece measures 6" from cast-on edge. Bind off. Then work front sts the same as back.

Sleeves
With dpns and color C2, CO 30sts. Pm and join ends, being careful not to twist the circle. Work in rev st st for 3 rnds. Add C1 and work Chart B. Continue in solid C1 until piece measures 4" from cast on edge. Bind off.

Finishing
Sew 5 sts at each shoulder. With C2 and dpns, pick up and knit each st for neck edge. Work 3 rows in rev st st. Bind off in purl. Attach sleeves and weave in ends.

Variation: Doll Sweater with Small Flowers and Picot Edge
(knit in the round)
Materials
Small amounts of #7808 (Purple Hyacinth; C1), #7814 (Chartreuse; C2) and #9438 (C3)
US 5 (3.75 mm) 16" (40 cm) circ ndl
US 7 (4.5 mm) 16" circ ndls, or size to obtain gauge
Set of matching dpns in both sizes

Directions
CO 72 sts with smaller circ ndl and C1. Pm and join ends, being careful not to twist the circle. Knit 3 rnds.
On the next rnd, *k2tog, yo, rep from *. Change to larger circ ndl and knit 3 rnds. At this point you can either keep knitting and whipstitch the hem in place once the sweater is complete, or you can knit the hem to the sweater as follows: fold the fabric at k2tog/yo row to create a picot edge. With a dpn, pick up each st along the cast-on edge (one at a time) and knit tog with the corresponding live st on your circ ndl. Continue around entire row.

Make small flowers as follows:
Rnd 1: * k1 with C1, k1 with C2, k4 with C1, rep from *

Rnd 2: *k1 with C1, knit in front and back of next st with C2 (this creates a 2-st increase as well as a horizontal bar which you will pick up on the next round to make the flower), k4 with C1, rep from *

Rnd 3: *k2tog with C1, pick up and knit the horizontal bar from the front with the right-hand ndl and knit it with C3, ssk with C1, k3 with C1, rep from *

Rnds 4-6: stagger the next row of flowers by beginning each rnd with k3 and working Rnds 1-3

(You may follow Chart C for rnds 1-6 above.)

Continue in solid C1 until piece measures 3" from edge. Place 35 sts on a holder (front) and work rem 35 sts (back) flat in st st until piece measures 6" from edge. Bind off. Then work front sts the same as back.

Sleeves
With smaller dpns and C1, CO 30 sts. Pm and join ends, being careful not to twist the circle. Knit 3 rnds. On the next rnd, *k2tog, yo, rep from *. Change to larger dpns and knit 3 rnds. Work Chart C. Continue in C1 until piece measures 4" from cast on-edge. Bind off.

Finishing
Sew 5 sts at each shoulder. With C1 and larger dpns, pick up and knit rem sts (must be an even number) for the collar. Knit 3 rnds. On the next rnd, *k2tog, yo, rep from *. Change to smaller dpns and knit 3 rnds. Bind off and whipstitch hem in place. Attach sleeves and weave in ends.

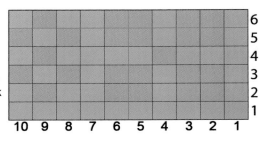

Chart B

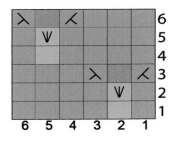

Chart C

- ssk
- k2tog
- incr - knit in front and back of st

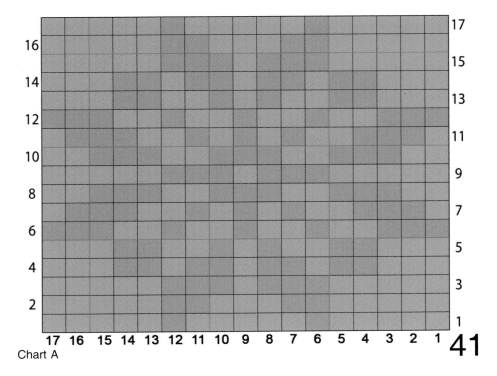

Chart A

Funnel Neck Sweaters
design by Urban Tribal Wear Designs

Finished sizes
S (M, L, XL)
Chest measurement 39 (42, 46, 49)"

Gauge
5.5 sts x 7rows = 1" worked in st st on larger ndl

Materials
7(8, 8, 9) skeins #8903 (Primaverra)
US 7 (4.5 mm) ndl
US 5 (3.75 mm) ndl

Directions
Front and Back
CO 102 (118, 126, 134) sts with smaller ndl. Work in k2, p2 rib for 3". Change to larger ndl and cont rib until piece measures 9 (9¼, 9½, 10)". Work in k1, p1 rib until piece measures 18 (18½, 19, 20)". Shape armholes as follows: working in k1,p1 rib, bind off 7 (10, 11, 12) sts at the beg of the next 2 rows, then dec 1 st each side every RS row 7 (10, 11, 12) times. Work even in rib until the piece measures 8 (8½, 9, 9½)" from armhole bind-off.

Shape shoulder and neck and follows: still working in k1, p1 rib, bind off 4 (5, 5, 5) sts at the beg of next 4 (6, 6, 2) rows. Bind off 5 (0, 0, 6) sts at beg of next 2 (0, 0, 4) rows. Work 48 (48, 52, 52) neck sts in k2, p2 rib until the funnel neck measures 103 . Bind off loosely in rib. Work a second piece for the back.

Sleeves
CO 46 (52, 52, 56) sts with smaller ndl. Work in k2, p2 rib for 2". Change to larger ndl and work until the cuff measures 10". Shape sleeves as follows: switching to k1, p1 rib, work one RS row. Inc 1 st on each side every RS row 12 (3, 7, 5) times, then every 4 rows 9 (19, 17, 19) times. Continue in rib until piece measures 19 (22½, 22½, 23)".

Shape cap: bind off 7 (10, 11, 12) sts at beg of next 2 rows. Dec 1 st each side every RS row 7 (10, 11, 12) times, dec 1 st each side *every* row 16 (13, 11, 9) times, then dec each side every 2 rows 0 (0, 1, 2) times. Bind off 3 (3, 4, 4) sts at beg of next 4 rows. Bind off rem 17 (18, 16, 18) sts.

Pattern 96

Finishing
Sew shoulders. Sew funnelneck on one side only, which allows it to lay open for different collar looks. Set in the sleeves and sew to armholes. Sew sleeves and side seams.

Variation: Two-Color Funnelneck with Seed Stitch Cuffs
Materials
5(6, 6, 7) skeins #9451 (Lake Chelan Heather; MC)
2 skeins #9461 (Lime Heather; CC)

Seed Stitch
Row 1: *k1, p1; rep from *, end k1.
Rep row 1.

Directions
Front and Back
CO 103 (119, 127, 135) sts with MC and smaller ndl. Work in seed st for 3". Change to larger ndl and cont in seed st until the piece measures 5 (5½, 6, 6½)". Change to CC and work in st st until the piece measures 10 (10½, 11, 12)". To shape armholes, bind off 7 (10, 11, 12) sts at the beg of the next 2 rows, then

dec 1 st each side every RS row 7 (10, 11, 12) times. Work even in st st until the piece measures 8 (8½, 9, 9½)" from armhole bind-off.

Shape shoulder and neck as described in the main pattern, but work shoulders in st st with CC. Switch to MC and work neck sts in seed st until funnelneck measures 4". Bind off loosely in seed stitch. Work a second piece for the back.

Sleeves
CO 47 (53, 53, 57) with MC and smaller ndl. Work in seed st for 2". Change to larger ndl and continue in seed st until the cuff measures 5". Switching to CC and st st, work one RS row. Shape sleeves as follows: inc 1 st on each side every RS row 12 (3, 7, 5) times, then every 4 rows 9 (19, 17, 19) times. Work until piece measures 14¼ (17½, 17½, 18)". Continuing in st st, shape cap as described in the main pattern. Finish as described in the main pattern.

Variation: Funnelneck Sweater with Shaped Waist and Flared Cuffs
Materials
6 (7, 8, 8) skeins

Directions
Front and Back
CO 102 (118, 126, 134) sts with smaller ndl. Work in 3" in st st. Change to larger ndl and work until the piece measures 5". Work k2, p2 rib until the piece measures 11 (11½, 12, 12½)". Work again in st st until the piece measures 14 (14½, 15, 15½)". Work armhole and shoulder shaping as described in the main pattern, but working in st st instead of rib. Work the 48 (48, 52, 52) neck sts in k1, p1 rib until the funnelneck measures 5" from beg. Bind off loosely in rib. Work a second piece for the front.

Sleeves
CO 88 (92, 94, 96) sts. Work in k1,p1 ribbing, decreasing 1 st each side every RS row 21 (21, 21, 22) times. When the piece measures 10", change to larger ndl. Work 1 RS row. Shape sleeves as follows: inc 1 st each side every RS row 12 (3, 7, 5) times, then every 4 rows 9 (19, 17, 19) times. Shape cap as described in the main pattern, binding off any rem sts. Finish as described in the main pattern.

Variation: Three-Color Funnelneck Sweater
Materials
2 skeins #2403 (Chocolate; Color 1)
2 (2, 2, 3) skeins #2414 (Ginger; Color 2)
3 (3, 4, 4) skeins #2415 (Sunflower; Color 3)

Directions
Front and Back
CO 102 (118, 126, 134) sts with smaller ndl and Color 1. Work in st st for 3". Change to larger ndl and work in st st until the piece measures 7 (7.25, 7.5, 7.75)". Change to Color 2 and work in st st until piece measures 14 (14.5, 15, 15.5)". Change to Color 3 and bind off 7 (10, 11, 12) sts at the beg of the next 2 rows. Dec 1 st each side every RS row 7 (10, 11, 12) times. Work in st st until the piece measures 8 (8.5, 9, 9.5)" from armhole bind-off.

Shape shoulders and neck as described in the main pattern, but work the neck sts for 5" in st st instead of ribbing. Bind off loosely. Make a second piece for the back.

Sleeves
CO 46 (52, 52, 56) sts with smaller ndl and Color 2. Work in st st for 2". Change to larger ndl and cont in st st until the cuff measures 6". Switch to Color 3 and work one RS row. Increase 1 st on each side every RS row 12 (3, 7, 5) times, then every 4 rows 9 (19, 17, 19) times. Continue in rib until piece measures 19 (22½, 22½, 23)". Shape caps as described in the main pattern. Finish as described in the main pattern.

Variation: Funnelneck Sweater with Cropped Sleeves
Materials
5 (6,6,7) skeins #8420 (Light Purple, Color 1)
2 skeins #2419 (Aster, Color 2)

Directions
Front and Back
CO 102 (118, 126, 134) sts with smaller ndl and Color 1. Work in garter st (knit every row) for 5". Change to larger ndl and Color 2. Work in st st until the piece measures 14 (14½, 15, 15½)". Work armhole, shoulder, and neck shaping as described in the main pattern, but instead of rib, work armholes and shoulders in st st, and the neck in garter st for 4". Bind off loosely. Make a second piece for the back.

Sleeves
CO 46 (50, 52, 52) sts with smaller ndl and Color 1. Work in garter st for 5". Switch to st st with larger ndl and Color 2. Work 1 RS row, then inc 1 st on each side every RS row 12 (12, 0, 11) times, every 4 rows 9 (10, 0, 13) times, then every 3 rows 0 (0, 24, 0) times. Continue in st st until the piece measures 14½ (15, 15½, 16½)". Shape cap in st st as described for the main pattern. Bind off any rem sts. Finish as described in the main pattern.

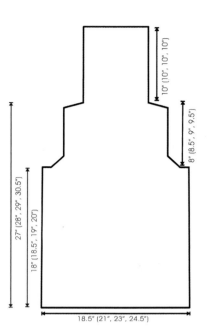

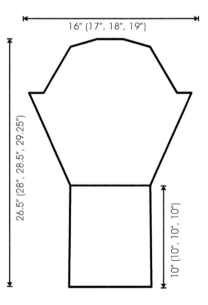

Button Top Hats

design by Elizabeth Wellenstein

Finished Sizes
S (M, L) 20 (22, 24)" circumference

Gauge
6 sts x 7 rows = 1" worked in 2-color knitting in the round.

Materials:
½ skein #2414 (Ginger, C1)
½ skein #2401 (Burgandy, C2)
½ skein #8885 (Dark Plum, C3)
½ skein #8229 (Country Green, C4)
US 5 (3.75 mm) 16" circ ndl or size to obtain gauge, 2 extra ndls for bind off
1 decorative button

Directions
CO 120 (132, 144) sts with C3. Pm and join ends, being careful not to twist the circle. Knit 15 rnds. Work Chart A until piece measures approx 7½ (8, 8½)" or desired length from chart row 1. Work last rnd ¾ of the way around to set up correct place to begin 3-needle bind off.

Finishing
Turn piece inside out. Place ½ of the sts on another ndl being careful to divide them so that the ndls run across your head (ends pointing ear to ear). Take a careful look to make sure you have the patterns on the front and back of the work aligned. Work 3-needle bind-off to end. Cut a 10" tail. Turn hat right side out and push out the corners created by the bind-off. Thread tail through tapestry needle and push it out through the corner. Then secure other corner with another stitch and add the button, centering it on top of the hat. Make a stitch in the top of the hat to secure the corners and the button there.

Variation: Color Hat with Hemmed Edge
Materials
1 skein #8892 (Teal, C1)
1 skein #8555 (Black, C2)
US 3 (3.25 mm) 16" circ ndl
US 5 (3.75 mm) 16" circ ndl

Directions
With C2 and smaller ndl, CO 120 (132, 144) sts. Pm and join ends, being careful not to twist the circle. Knit 6 rnds. Purl 1 rnd. Change to larger ndl. Knit 3 rnds. Work Chart B, repeating rows 21-32 until

Pattern 102

desired length. Finish as described in main pattern. Whipstitch hem in place.

Variation: Woven Stitch Hat with Rolled Edge
Materials
1 skein, #8229 (Country Green)

Woven Stitch
Rnd 1: *k1, sl 1 wyif; rep from *
Rnds 2 and 4: knit
Rnd 3: *sl 1 wyif, k1; rep from *

Directions
CO 120 (132, 144) sts. Pm and join ends, being careful not to twist the circle. Knit 15 rnds. Work woven st until piece measures desired length. Finish as described in the main pattern.

Variation: Jester Hat with Cables
Finished sizes
S (M, L) 19 (21, 23)" circumference

Gauge
6 sts x 8 rows = 1" worked in cable pattern in the round with larger ndl

Materials
1 skein, #7823 (Gold)
US 4 (3.5 mm) 16" circ ndl
US 6 (4.25 mm) 16" circ ndl, or size to obtain gauge.

Rib Stitch
Rnd 1: * k2, p2, k2, p1, rep from *
Rep rnd 1.

4-Stitch Cable
Rnd 1: * k2, c4f, p1, rep from *
Rnds 2 and 4: * k6, p1, rep from *
Rnd 3: *c4b, k2, p1, rep from *

Directions
With smaller ndls, CO 112 (126, 140) sts. Pm and join work, being careful not to twist the circle. Work Rib Stitch for 4 rnds. Change to larger ndl and work 4-Stitch Cable until desired length. Finish as described in the main pattern, but instead of attaching corners to center of hat, add pom-poms or tassles to each tip.

Variation: Geometric Jester Hat with Rolled Edge
Finished sizes 20 (22, 24)"

Materials
½ skein #8555 (Black, C1)
½ skein #2414 (Ginger, C2)
½ skein #2401 (Burgandy, C3)
½ skein #8885 (Dark Plum, C4)

Directions
CO 120 (132, 144) with C1. Pm and join ends, being careful not to twist the circle. Knit 15 rnds. Work Chart C until desired length. Finish as described in the main pattern, but instead of attaching corners to center of hat, add pom-poms or tassles to each tip.

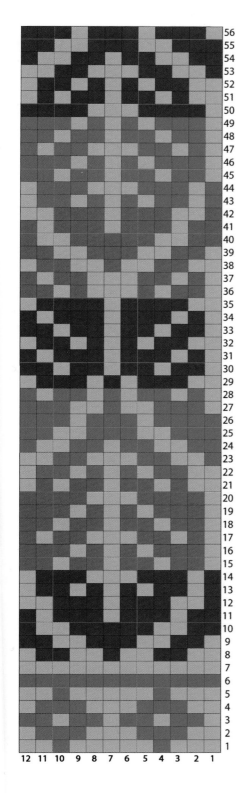

Chart A

Pattern 104

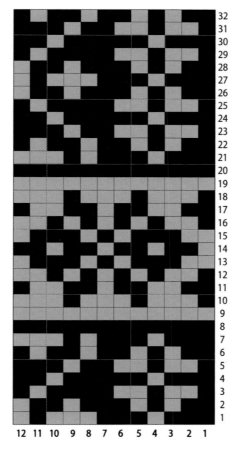

Chart B

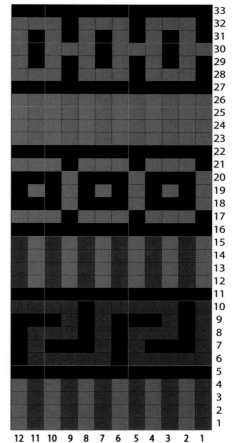

Chart C

45

Dolman Sleeve Sweaters

design by Urban Tribal Wear Designs

Finished sizes
Chest measurement 32 (36, 40, 44)"

Gauge
5.5 sts x 7 rows = 1" worked in st st with larger ndl

Materials
5 (6, 7, 7) skeins #7803 (Magenta)
US 7 (4.5 mm) 24" circ ndl
US 6 (4.0 mm) 24" circ ndl

Directions
CO 88 (100, 112, 124) sts with larger ndl. Work in k2, p2 ribbing for 8". Change to st st and shape sleeves as follows: CO 10 sts at the beg of the next 2 rows, CO 6 sts at the beg of the next 24 rows, then CO 7 sts at beg of next 2 rows. Work even until cuff edge measures 4¼". Bind off loosely. Make a second piece.

Sew the top of the sleeve 19" in from each cuff, leaving a 10 (12, 14, 16)" neck opening. Sew on the RS, so the seam is exposed along the top of the sleeve. With smaller ndl and RS facing, pick up 54 sts along cuff and work back and forth in st st until the cuff measures 3" (this forms a rolled cuff). Sew under sleeves and along sides from WS.

Pattern 106

Variation: Two-Color Dolman Pullover
Materials
4 (5, 6, 6) skeins #2414 (Ginger; MC)
1 skein #2411 (Café; CC)

Directions
Work sweater as described in the main pattern, working the ribbing in CC, and changing to MC for the remainder of the body. Sew shoulders as described. With smaller ndl and RS facing, pick up 54 sts with CC at cuff edge. Work back and forth in k2, p2 rib for 4". Bind off loosely in rib. With smaller ndl and RS facing, pick up 55 (66, 77, 88) sts with CC along front neck edge and 55 (66, 77, 88) sts along back neck edge, pm, and join. Work in k1, p1 ribin the rnd for 2". Bind off loosely in rib.

Variation: Dolman Pullover with a Deep-Folded Cuff
Materials
6 skeins MC
1 skein CC

Directions
Work sweater as described in the main pattern, working the rib in CC, and changing to MC for the remainder of the body. Sew shoulders as described. With smaller ndl, pick up 54 sts with CC along neck. Work back and forth in k2, p2 rib for 10". Bind off loosely in rib.

Variation: One-Piece Dolman Sweater
Materials
5 (6, 7, 7) skeins

Directions
Work dolman sweater as described in the main pattern, but do not bind off. Knit 89 sleeve sts and 15 shoulder sts, join a second ball of yarn, then bind off 55 (66, 77, 88) neck sts. Work to end of row. Working both sides at once, work 1 WS row to neck. CO 55 (66, 77, 88) neck sts and work even until the cuff edge measures 8½".

Shape sleeves to correspond with the back arm shaping as follows: bind off 10 sts at the beg of the next 2 rows, bind off 6 sts at the beg of the next 24 rows, then bind off 7 sts at the beg of the next 2 rows. Work k2, p2 rib for 8". Bind off loosely in rib.

Work cuffs as described in the main pattern. Fold garment in half and seam under sleeves and sides. Finish neck as desired.

Variation: Three-Quarter Sleeve Dolman with a Cowl Neck
Materials
6 skeins #8012 (Doeskin Heather; MC)
1 skein #9324 (Misty Lilac Heather; CC)

Directions
With MC, work body in two pieces as in the main pattern, or in one piece as in #109. With smaller ndl and RS facing, pick up 55 (66, 77, 88) sts with CC along front neck edge and 55 (66, 77, 88) sts along back neck edge. Pm, join, and work in k1, p1 rib in the rnd for 6". Change to larger ndl and work another 6". Bind off loosely in rib. Another option is a 4" fringe around neck edge and cuffs.

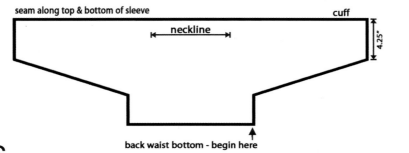

seam along top & bottom of sleeve — cuff — neckline — 4.25" — back waist bottom - begin here

Legwarmers
design by Elizabeth Wellenstein

Finished size
12" in circumference, 12" long.
Note: instructions on how to adjust size are given in each pattern.

Gauge
5 sts x 7 rows = 1" worked in st st in the rnd

Materials
1 skein #8415 (Cranberry)
Set of US 7 (4.5 mm) dpns

Directions
CO 60 sts. Pm and join ends, being careful not to twist the circle. Knit in st st (knit every rnd) for 7 rnds. Work k2, p2 rib for 6 rnds. Work st st for 8". Work k2, p2 ribbing for 6 rnds. Work 6 rnds in st st. Bind off and weave in ends. To adjust size, inc or dec in increments of 4 sts (the pattern repeat for the rib).

Diamond Rib Legwarmers
Materials
1 skein #8888 (Lavender)

Directions
CO 60 sts. Pm and join ends, being careful not to twist the circle. Knit in st st for 7 rnds. Work Chart A for approx 10". Work 7 rnds st st. Work k2, p2 rib for 6 rnds. Work 6 rnds in st st. Bind off and weave in ends. To increase size, add another column of purl sts between diamonds.

Lace Rib Legwarmers
Materials
1 skein #9456 (Sapphire Heather)

Lace Rib
Rnd 1: *p2, yo, k2tog tbl, k1; rep from *
Rnd 2 and every alt rnd: *p2, k3; rep from *
Rnd 3: *p2, k1, yo, k2tog tbl; rep from *

Directions
CO 60 sts. Pm and join ends, being careful not to twist the circle. Knit in st st for 7 rnds. Work Lace Rib for approx 10". Work 7 rnds st st. Work k2, p2 rib for 6 rnds. Work 6 rnds in st st. Bind off and weave in ends. To adjust size, inc or dec in increments of 5 sts (the pattern repeat for the lace).

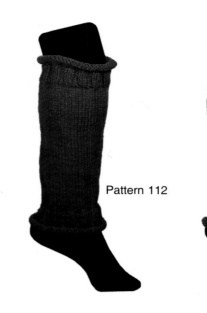

Pattern 112

Pattern 115

Chart A

☐ knit
▪ purl

Chart B

☐ knit
▪ purl

Spiral Rib Legwarmers
Materials
1 skein #9457 (Cobalt Heather)

Directions
CO 60 sts. Pm and join ends, being careful not to twist the circle. Knit in st st for 7 rnds. Work Chart B for approx 10". Work 7 rnds st st. Work k2, p2 rib for 6 rnds. Work 6 rnds in st st. Bind off and weave in ends. To adjust size, inc or dec in increments of 6 sts.

Fish Tail Legwarmers
Materials
1 skein #9419 (Vermeer Blue)

Fish Tail Panel
Rnd 1: * p1, yo, k4, k3tog, k4, yo, p1, k17; rep from *
Rnd 2 and all alt rnds: knit the knit sts (including yo) and purl the purl sts
Rnd 3: * p1, k1, yo, k3, k3tog, k3, yo, k1, p1, k17; rep from *

Rnd 5: * p1, k2, yo, k2, k3tog, k2, yo, k2, p1, k17; rep from *
Rnd 7: * p1, k3, yo, k1, k3tog, k1, yo, k3, p1, k17; rep from *
Rnd 9: * p1, k4, yo, k3tog, yo, k4, p1, k17; rep from *
Rnd 10: as rnd 2.

Directions
CO 60 sts. Pm and join ends, being careful not to twist the circle. Knit in st st for 7 rnds. Work Rows 1-10 of Fish Tail Panel 5 times. Work 7 rnds st st. Work k2, p2 rib for 6 rnds. Work 6 rnds in st st. Bind off and weave in ends. To adjust size, inc or dec in the st st between panels.

47

Ponchos

design by Urban Tribal Wear Designs

Pattern 116

Finished Size
One size fits most

Gauge
5.5 sts x 7 rows = 1" worked in st st

Materials
2 skeins each #2410(Deep Purple; C1), #7807 (Med. Purple; C2), #7808 (Lavender; C3), #7802 (Lite Pink; C4), and #7803 (Magenta; C5)
US 7 (4.5 mm) 24" circ ndl

Directions
CO 32 sts with C1. Work Chart A. When piece measures 30" bind off very loosely (it is easiest to sew together if the bound off edge is as loose as the knitted piece). Make a second piece – they look terrific if the pattern doesn't match perfectly on both sides, so pick up where you left off on the pattern instead of making 2 identical pieces.

Embroider freehand across lines 11-18 using C5. *Hint:* lay out the embroidery pattern using scrap yarn, pin it in place, then stem stitch along side the guide yarn. When done with embroidery, remove guide yarn and add french knots as embellishment. Weave in all ends and sew together as shown in Diagram 1.

Variation: Leaf Lace Poncho
Materials
8 skeins #8914 (Citron) or #9466 (Persimmon)

Leaf Lace
Row 1 (and all WS rows): purl
Row 2: k3, *k2tog, yo, k1, yo, ssk, k5, rep from *; end k3
Row 4: k2, *k2tog, [k1, yo] twice, k1, ssk, k3, rep from *; end k2
Row 6: k1, *k2tog, k2, yo, k1, yo, k2, ssk, k1, rep from *
Row 8: k2tog, *k3, yo, k1, yo, k3, sl 1, k2tog, psso, rep from * to last 9 sts; end with k3, yo, k1, yo, k3, ssk
Row 10: k1 *yo, ssk, k5, k2tog, yo, k1, rep from *
Row 12: k1, *yo, k1, ssk, k3, k2tog, k1, yo, k1, rep from *
Row 14: k1, *yo, k2, ssk, k1, k2tog, k2, yo, k1, rep from *
Row 16: k1, *yo, k3, sl1, k2tog, psso, k3, yo, k1, rep from *

Directions
CO 131 sts. Work Leaf Lace until piece measures approx 30". Bind off very loosely, so that the bind off stretches as

well as the body of the piece. Make a second identical piece. Sew together as shown in Diagram 1.

Variation: Poncho with a Cowl Neck
Materials
8 skeins #9442 (Baby Rose Heather)
US 7 (4.5 mm) 24" circ ndl
US 6 (4.0 mm) 24" circ ndl

Pattern Stitch
Row 1: (RS): k1, *yo, k8, k2tog, rep from *; end k1
Row 2: p1, *p2tog, p7, yo, p1, rep from *; end p1
Row 3: k1, *k2, yo, k6, k2tog, rep from *; end k1
Row 4: p1, *p2tog, p5, yo, p3, rep from *; end p1
Row 5: k1, *k4, yo, k4, k2tog, rep from *; end k1
Row 6: p1, *p2tog, p3, yo, p5, rep from *; end p1
Row 7: k1, *k6, yo, k2, k2tog, rep from *; end k1
Row 8: p1, *p2tog, p1, yo, p7, rep from *; end p1
Row 9: k1, *k8, yo, k2tog, rep from *; end k1
Row 10: p1, *yo, p8, p2tog tbl, rep from*; end p1
Row 11: k1, *ssk, k7, yo, k1, rep from *; end k1
Row 12: p1, *p2, yo, p6, p2tog tbl, rep from *; end p1
Row 13: K1, *ssk, k5, yo, k3, rep from *; end k1
Row 14: p1, *p4, yo, p4, p2tog tbl, rep from *; end p1

Row 15: k1, *ssk, k3, yo, k5; rep from *; end k1
Row 16: p1, *p6, yo, p2, p2tog tbl, rep from *; end p1
Row 17: k1, *ssk, k1, yo, k7; rep from *; end k1
Row 18: p1, *p8, yo, p2tog tbl, rep from *; end p1

Directions
CO 132 sts. Work Pattern Stitch 12 times. Bind off very loosely. Make a second piece and sew pieces together as shown in Diagram 1. Using smaller ndl and with RS facing, pick up sts evenly around the neck opening and work k1, p1 rib for 12". Bind off loosely in rib.

Add a 4" fringe around the bottom of the neck if desired as well as an 8" fringe around the bottom of the poncho. *Note:* 4" fringe = 8" piece of yarn; 8" fringe = 16" piece of yarn

Variation: Cabled Poncho
Materials
8 skeins #9451 (Lake Chelan Heather)

Cable Pattern
Row 1 (WS): k1, *p1, k4, p4, k4, p1, rep from *; end, k1
Row 2: p1, k1 tbl, *p4, c4f, p4, c2f, rep from * to last 2 sts; end k1 tbl, p1
Row 3 and all other WS rows: knit the knit sts and purl the purl sts
Row 4: p1, *sfc, p2, bc, fc, p2, sbc, rep from *; end p1
Row 6: p1, *p1, sfc, bc, p2, fc, sbc, p1, rep from *; end p1

48

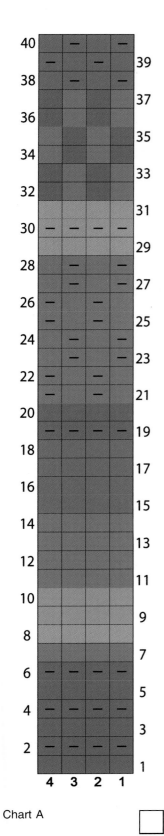

Chart A

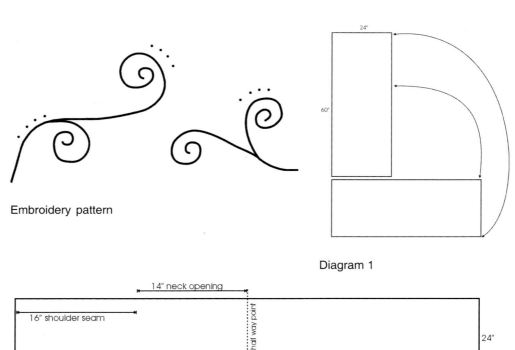

Embroidery pattern

Diagram 1

Diagram 2

14" neck opening

16" shoulder seam

fold line - half way point

60"

24"

Row 8: p1, *p2, bkc, p4, fkc, p2, rep from *; end p1
Row 10: p1*, p1, bc, sfc, p2, sbc, fc, p1, rep from *; end p1
Row 12: p1, *bc, p2, sfc, sbc, p2, fc, rep from *; end p1
Row 14: p1, k2, *p4, sl 1 onto cable ndl and hold in back, k1 tbl, k1 tbl from cable ndl, p4, c4b, rep from * to last 3 sts; end k2, p1
Row 16: p1, *fc, p2, sbc, sfc, p2, bc, rep from *; end p1
Row 18: p1, *p1, fc, sbc, p2, sfc, bc, p1, rep from *; end p1
Row 20: p1, *p2, fkc, p4, bkc, p2, rep from *; end p1
Row 22: p1, *p1, sbc, fc, p2, bc, sfc, p1, rep from *; end p1
Row 24: p1, *sbc, p2, fc, bc, p2, sfc, rep from *; end p1

tbl: through back loop
C4F: sl 2 sts onto cable ndl and hold in front, knit next 2 sts, knit 2 from cable ndl
C4B: sl 2 sts onto cable ndl and hold in back, knit next 2 sts, knit 2 from cable ndl
C2F: sl 1 st onto cable ndl and hold in front, knit next st tbl, knit 1 tbl from cable needle

SFC : sl 1 onto cable ndl and hold in front, p1, k1 tbl from cable ndl
BC : sl 1 st to cable needle and hold in back, k2, then p1 from cable needle.
FC: sl 2 to cable ndl and hold in front, p1, k2 from cable ndl
SBC: sl 1 to cable ndl and hold in back, k1 tbl, p1 from cable ndl
BKC: sl 1 to cable ndl and hold in back, k2, then k1 tbl from cable ndl
FKC: sl 2 onto cable ndl and hold in front, k1 tbl, k2 from cable ndl

Directions
Cast on 156 sts. Work Cable Pattern 9 times or until pieces measures 30". Make a second piece and sew pieces together as shown in Diagram 1.

Variation: Shawl or Asymmetrical Poncho
This piece is 24" x 60" (or longer) in a single rectangle. It can be folded in half and stitched together along the "shoulder", leaving a neck opening.

Directions
Choose any of the poncho patterns. Work one piece to 60" length. Fold and stitch as shown in Diagram 2.

☐ **knit**
─ **purl**

49

Cowl Scarves

design by Urban Tribal Wear Designs

Gauge
5.5 sts x 7 rows = 1"

Materials
3 skeins of contrasting colors (C1, C2, C3)
US 7 (4.5 mm) 24" circ ndl

Directions
With C1, CO 208 sts. Pm and join, being careful not to twist the circle. Work Chart A pattern for 9". Change to C2 and continue in pattern for 9". Change to C3 and continue in pattern for 9". Bind off loosely in pattern.

Variation: Garter Stitch Cowl with Points
Materials
1 skein each (C1), (C2)

Directions
CO 2 sts with C1. *Turn, inc in first st, k to end, repeat from * until there are 8 sts total. Break yarn, leaving sts on ndl. Rep until there are 26 points. Pm and join, being careful not to twist the circle. Work even in garter stitch (knit one rnd, purl one rnd) for 3". Change to C2 and work in st st (knit all rounds) for 21". Change to C1 and work in garter stitch again for 3".

On next rnd, k8, *turn, k2tog, k to end, repeat from * until there are 2 sts left. Bind off. Repeat until all 26 points have been worked and bound off. Tie beads to the ends of the points, if desired.

Variation: Drop Stitch Cowl
Materials
3 skeins #8229 (Country Green)

Drop Stitch
Rnd 1: *k1, m1, k1, p2, k2, p2, rep from * to end of rnd
Rnd 2-6: *k3, p2, k2, p2, rep from *
Rnd 7: *k1, drop one st and unravel, k1, p2, k1, m1, k1, p2, rep from *
Rnd 8-12: *k2, p2, k3, p2, rep from *
Rnd 13: k1, m1, k1, p2, k1, drop one st and unravel, k1, p2, rep from *

CO 208 sts. Pm and join, being careful not to twist the circle. Work Rnd 1-13 of Drop Stitch pattern. Then work Rnds 2-13

Pattern 123

of Drop Stitch pattern until the piece measures approx 27½", ending with row 13.

On the next rnd, * k1, drop 1, p2, k2, p2, rep from * to end of rnd. Knit one rnd. Bind off loosely.

Rebecca Cowl
Materials
½ skein each #9419 (Vermeer Blue; C1), #8903 (Primaverra; C2), #9469 (Hot Pink; C3), #7825 (Orange Sherbet; C4), #7809 (Violet; C5), and #8901 (Groseille; C6).

Directions
CO 208 sts. Pm and join, being careful not to twist the circle. With C5, work 4" in seed stitch. Work Chart B twice, then work Chart B twice more in reverse. With C5, work 4" in seed stitch. Bind off loosely in seed stitch.

Striped Cowl
Materials
3 skeins of contrasting colors (C1, C2, C3)

Directions
CO 208 sts with C1 and join, being careful not to twist the circle. Work in st st

for 2". Purl one rnd. Work in st st for 2½" (this forms the finished edge - fold over at purl rnd and slip stitch in place to keep from rolling too much). Continue in st st, work 1 rnd in C1, work 1 rnd in C2, work 1 rnd in C3. Repeat these 3 rnds, carrying the colors up the inside.

When the piece measures 27", work 2½" in C1. Purl one rnd. Work 2" in st st. Bind off loosely. Fold in the edge and slip stitch in place.

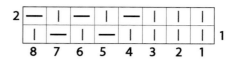

Chart A

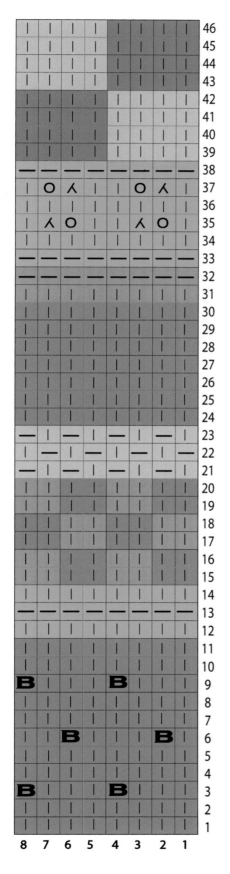

8 7 6 5 4 3 2 1

Chart B

Pattern 123

| | knit

− purl

人 k2tog

O yo

B make bobble
k, p, k in the next stitch. turn.
p3, turn, k3, turn, p3, turn k3.

Medieval Hooded Scarves

design by Urban Tribal Wear Designs

Finished size
36" on each side of hood

Gauge
5.5 sts x 7 rows = 1" worked in st st

Materials
5 skeins #8013 (Walnut Heather)
US 7 (4.5 mm) ndl

Seed Stitch
Row 1: *k1, p1; rep from *, end k1
Rep row 1.

Dragon Skin
Row 1 (and all other WS rows): purl
Row 2: *k1, m1, ssk, k4, k2tog, k3, m1, k2, m1, k3, ssk, k4, k2tog, m1, k1, rep from *
Row 4: *k1, m1, k1, ssk, k2, k2tog, k4, m1, k2, m1, k4, ssk, k2, k2tog, k1, m1, k1, rep from *
Row 6: *k1, m1, k2, ssk, k2tog, k5, m1, k2, m1, k5, ssk, k2tog, k2, m1, k1, rep from *
Row 8: *k1, m1, k3, ssk, k4, k2tog, m1, k2, m1, ssk, k4, k2tog, k3, m1, k1, rep from *
Row 10: *k1, m1, k4, ssk, k2, k2tog, k1, m1, k2, m1, k1, ssk, k2, k2tog, k4, m1, k1, rep from *
Row 12: *k1, m1, k5, ssk, k2tog, k2, (m1, k2) twice, ssk, k2tog, k5, m1, k1, rep from *

Directions

Scarf
CO 530 sts. Work 5 sts in seed stitch, pm, work in Dragon Skin to last 5 sts, pm, work last 5 sts in seed stitch. Work back and forth in this manner for 4 pattern repeats. Bind off 208 sts, work to end, bind off 208 sts, and work to end (114 sts remain).

Hood
Foundation row: work 5 st in seed stitch, pm, k52, pm, m1 (center seam), pm, k52, pm, work 5 st in seed stitch (115 sts). Begin working in seed stitch and Dragon Skin pattern.

When the pieces measures 3½" begin hood shaping as follows: m1 on each side of the center stitch, *work 3 rows, on the next row, work to center marker, slip marker, m1, work to next center marker, m1, slip marker, resume pattern. Rep from * 2 more times.

Increase in the same manner every 5 rows 9 times. Work in pattern until the piece measures 13½". Bind off all sts and sew center hood seam. Alternatively, using using circ ndl, fold the remaining sts in half with RS facing and bind off sts using the 3-needle bind-off method.

Pattern 126

Variation: Seed Stitch Hooded Scarf
Seed Stitch
Row 1: *k1, p1; rep from *, end k1.
Rep row 1.

Materials
5 skeins #2433 (Pacific)

Directions
Cast on 531 sts. Work scarf and hood in seed stitch.

Variation: Madeira Leaf Scarf
Materials
5 skeins #9441(Mauve Heather)

Madeira Leaf
Row 1, 2, 3, 5 (RS): knit
Row 4 and 6: purl
Row 7: k2 *yo ssk, k8, rep from *; end k2
Row 8: p9, *p2 tog tbl, yo, p8, rep from *; end p3
Row 9: k2, *(yo, ssk) twice, k6, rep from *; end p5
Row 10: p7, *p2 tog tbl, yo, p8, rep from *; end p5
Row 11: k2, *(k1, yo, ssk) twice, k4, rep from *; end k2
Row 12: p5, *p2 tog tbl, yo, p8, rep from *; end p7
Row 13: k2, *(k2, yo, ssk) twice, k2, rep from *; end k2
Row 14: p3, *p2 tog tbl, yo, p8, rep from *; end p1
Row 15: k2, *(k3, yo, ssk) twice, rep from *; end k2
Row 16: p6, *p2 tog tbl, yo, p8, rep from *; end p6
Row 17: k3, *k4, yo, ssk, k2, yo, ssk, rep from *; end k1
Row 18: p4, *p2 tog tbl yo, p8, rep from *
Row 19: k2, *yo, ssk, k5, yo, ssk, k1, rep from *; end k2
Row 20: p2, *p2 tog tbl, yo, p8, rep from *; end p2
Row 21: k3, *yo, ssk, k6, yo, ssk, rep from *; end k1
Row 22: p10, *p2 tog tbl, yo, p8, rep from *; end p2
Row 23: k3, *yo, ssk, k8, rep from *; end k1
Row 24: knit
Row 25: k2, *yo, ssk, rep from *; end k2
Row 26: knit
Row 27: k2, *k2 tog, yo, k8, rep from *; end k2
Row 28: p1, *yo, p2 tog, p8, rep from *; end p1
Row 29: k2, *p2tog, yo, k6, k2tog, yo, rep from *; end k2
Row 30: p3, *yo, p2 tog, p8, rep from *; end p1
Row 31: k1, *k2 tog, yo, k5, k2tog, yo, k1, rep from *; end k3

Row 32: p6, *yo, p2tog, p8, rep from *; end p7
Row 33: k2, *k4, k2tog, yo, k2, k2tog, yo, rep from * end k2
Row 34: p7, * yo, p2tog, p8, rep from * end p5
Row 35: k1, *(k3, k2tog, yo) twice, rep from *; end k3
Row 36: p4, *yo, p2tog, p8, rep from *
Row 37: k3, *k2tog, yo, k2, k2tog, yo, k4, rep from *; end k1
Row 38: p6, *yo, p2tog, p8, rep from *; end p6
Row 39: k2, * k2tog, yo, k1, k2tog, yo, k5, rep from *; end k2
Row 40: p8, *yo, p2tog, p8, rep from *; end p4
Row 41: k1, *(k2tog, yo) twice, k6, rep from *; end k3
Row 42: p10, *yo, p2tog, p8, rep from *; end p2
Row 43: k1, *k2 tog, yo, k8, rep from *; end k3
Row 44: purl
Row 45-49: knit

Directions
CO 534 sts. Work 5 sts in garter stitch (knit all sts), pm, work in pattern to last 5 sts, pm, work last 5 sts in garter stitch. Work scarf in Madeira Leaf pattern, keeping the first 5 and last 5 sts in garter stitch throughout. When rows 1-49 are complete, bind off 210 sts at the beg of the next 2 rows.

Work the hood as described in the main pattern, using garter stitch for the first 5 and last 5 sts of the hood and st st for the body of the hood.

Variation: Urban Tribal Ribbed Hooded Scarf
Materials
5 skeins #8013 (Walnut Heather)

Directions
Work scarf and hood as described in the main pattern, but substitute the textured pattern in Chart A. Maintain seed stitch at the ends and along the edge of the hood.

Variation: Stockinette Hood with Dragonscale Scarf in Two Colors
Materials
2 skein #8914 (Granny Smith; MC)
3 skeins #8911 (Grape Jelly; CC)

Directions
With MC, work the scarf as described in the main pattern. Change to CC and work the hood in st st (knit one row, purl one row), keeping 5 sts in seed stitch along edges.

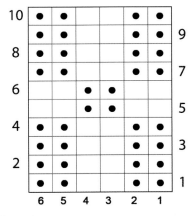

Chart A

· knit on right side, purl on wrong side

☐ purl on right side, knit on wrong side

Mens Vests

design by Urban Tribal Wear Designs

Finished Sizes
Men's size 40 (42, 44, 46)"
Chest measurement 43 (45, 47, 49)"

Gauge
5.5 sts x 7 rows = 1" worked in st st on larger ndl

Materials
5 (5, 5, 6) skeins #8509 (Grey)
US 7 (4.5 mm) 243 circ ndl
US 6 (4.0 mm) 163 circ ndl or dpns

Directions
Back
CO 118 (125, 129, 135) sts with smaller ndl. Work in k3, p1 rib for 2½ (2½, 3, 3)". Change to larger ndl and continue in st st until piece measures 15½ (16, 16, 16½)". Shape armholes as follows: bind off 6 (7, 8, 8) sts at beg of next 2 rows, then dec 1 st on each side every RS row 6 (7, 7, 8) times. Work even until piece measures 8½, (9, 9½, 10)" from armhole bind off.

Shape shoulders and back neck
Bind off 9 (9, 10, 10) sts at beg of next row, work across. At beg of next row, bind off 9 (9, 10, 10) sts. Work 18 (18, 19, 20) sts, attach a second ball of yarn, and bind off 38 (40, 41, 43) sts for the back of neck. Complete row. Working both sides at once, bind off 9 (9, 9, 10) sts at the beginning of each armhole edge and dec 1 st at each neck edge. Bind off 9 (9, 9, 10) sts at the beg of the next row. Bind off 9 sts at the beg of the next 2 rows.

Front
Work as for back, including all shaping. When the piece measures 16½ (17, 17, 17½)" , begin V-neck shaping as follows: work to center, attach another ball of yarn, and complete row. Working both sides at once, dec 1 st on each neck edge every RS row 13 (14, 12, 12) times, then every 4 rows 7 (7, 9, 10) times. Continue working even until the piece measures 8½, (9, 9½, 10)" from the armhole bind-off. Shape shoulders to correspond with back.

Finishing
Neck
Sew shoulder and side seams. With smaller ndl and RS facing, pick up and knit 49 (50, 54, 54) sts from the right neck, 46 (48, 49, 49) sts from the back neck, and 49 (50, 54, 54) sts from the left neck. Turn. Work back and forth in k1, p1 rib for 1". Bind off loosely in rib. Sew the

edge of the V-neck into place (the two pieces will overlap).

Armhole
Pick up and knit 104 (110, 116, 122) sts evenly around armhole. Pm, join, and work in k1, p1 rib in the rnd for ¾".

Variation: Seed Stitch Diamond Vest
Materials
5 (5, 5, 6) skeins #9408 (Cordovan)

Directions
Work basic vest as described in the main pattern. Work the back piece in st st. When the front piece measures 12¼ (12¾, 12¾, 13½)", work Chart A, beginning at your size, and reversing to work the mirror half of the pattern. Finish as described in the main pattern.

Variation: Diamond Fair Isle Vest
Materials
5 (5, 5, 6) skeins #8400 (Charcoal Grey; MC)
1 skein #8891 (Turquoise; CC1)
small amount of #8910 (Citron; CC2)

Directions
Work vest in MC as described in the main pattern. Work the back piece in MC. When the front piece measures 12¼ (12¾, 12¾, 13½)", work Chart B in MC

and CC1, beginning at your size, and reversing to work the mirror half of the pattern. Work the third color (blue on pattern) in duplicate stitch with CC2. Finish as described in the main pattern, using CC for the neck trim and MC for the sleeve trim.

Variation: Fair Isle Vest
Materials
5 (5, 5, 6) skeins #8908 (Anis; MC)
1 skein #8884 (Claret; CC1)
1 skein #8686 (Brown; CC2)
1 skein #2433 (Pacific; CC3)

Directions
Work basic vest as described in the main pattern. Work the back piece in MC. When the front piece measures 12¼ (12¾, 12¾, 13½)" , work Chart C in MC , CC1, and CC2, beginning at your size, and reversing to work the mirror half of the pattern. Work the fourth color in duplicate stitch with CC3. Work neck trim in CC3 and armhole trim in MC.

Variation: Textured Vest
Materials

5 (5, 5, 6) skeins

Directions

Work basic vest as described in the main pattern. Work the back piece in st st. When the front piece measures 12¼ (12¾, 12¾, 13½)", work Chart D, beginning at your size, and reversing to work the mirror half of the pattern. Finish as described in the main pattern.

Variation: Vest with Shawl Collar
Materials

5 (5, 5, 6) skeins #2438 (Spring Meadow)

Directions

Work vest back and front as described in the main pattern and sew pieces together. With smaller ndl and RS facing, pick up 49 (50, 54, 57) sts from right neck edge (starting in the center V), pick up 38 (40, 41, 43) back neck sts, and 49 (50, 54, 57) left neck sts. Turn. Work 32 (33, 34, 36) sts in k1, p1 rib, pm, work 72 (74, 81, 85) sts in k1, p1 rib, pm, turn.

Begin short rows

*work back to opposite marker, remove marker, wrap (sl next st wyif if a knit st, or with yarn in back if a purl st; return yarn to back or front), pm on left needle, and return the sl st to the left ndl), turn. Rep from * until 8 sts rem on either side of center V.

Work back to right marker, remove marker, continue working sts to within 2 sts of center, ssk, pm, k1 (center st), k2tog. Continue in the rnd, decreasing 1 st on each side of the center marker 8 times. Work 1". Bind off loosely.

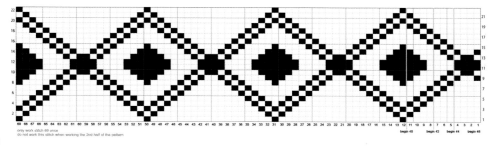

Chart A

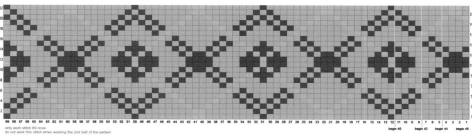

Chart B

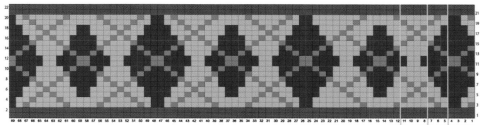

Chart C

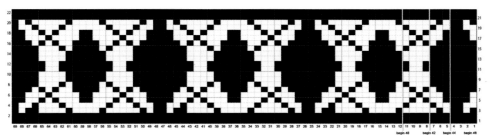

Chart D

■ knit on right side, purl on wrong side
■ purl on right side, knit on wrong side

55

Cap Sleeve Shell

design by Patti Pierce Stone

Finished sizes
S (M, L) measures 37, 40, 43"

Gauge
20sts x 24rows = 4" worked in st st

Materials
5 (6, 6) skeins #9421 (Blue Hawaii)
US 7 (4.5 mm) 24" (60 cm) circ needle
US F crochet hook

Double Moss (multiple of 4 st + 2)
Rows 1 and 2: *k2, p2, rep from *; end k2
Rows 3 and 4: *p2, k2, rep from *; end p2

rvs sc: reverse single crochet

Directions
Yoke
CO 86 (90, 94) sts and join. Work in garter st (knit one rnd, purl one rnd) for 6 rnds. On the next rnd, knit to end, turn, and knit transition row as follows: *p18 (18, 20), m1, p17 (18, 18), m1* rep from * 3 times, purl to last stitch, turn (90, 94, 98 st). Working back and forth, continue in Double Moss pattern for 28 (32, 34) rows (4½, 5¼, 5¾" from cuff)

Split for neck
Work in Double Moss for 44 (46, 48) sts. Cast off next 2 sts to split for neck. Work in Double Moss to end of row. Turn. Work Double Moss for 58 (58, 62) rows from beginning of neck. On the next WS row, attach a second ball of yarn and work the sts on the other side of the split. The neck opening is about 9½ (9½, 10)" from the beginning of the split.

Rejoin shoulder
Work the next row of Double Moss to the split. CO 2 sts. Continue in Double Moss across the second shoulder to join. Continue working in Double Moss until piece measures 4½ (5¼, 5¾)" from the neck opening.

Cuff
On next row, p17 (17, 19), k2tog, *p16 (17, 17), k2tog*, rep from * to * 3 times, purl to last st, turn (86, 90, 94 sts). Knit across and join to form a circle. The remainder of the yoke will be worked in the rnd. Work garter st (knit one rnd, purl one rnd) for 6 rnds, beginning with a purl rnd. Bind off evenly.

Pattern 141

Body
Pm where each underarm is joined. Join yarn at left side and pick up 94 (100, 108) sts between markers (about 4 sts for every 5 rows). Repeat for the back (188, 200, 216 sts). Be sure to pick up one st in each "corner" at the underarm, between the front and back.

Knit one rnd, then work a decrease rnd as follows: k2, k2tog, k to 4 sts before next marker, ssk, k2. Repeat for back of sweater. Work dec rnd every other rnd 2 more times (12 sts dec; 176, 188, 204 sts remain). Knit even until sweater is 12 (13, 14)" from yoke or 1¼" shorter than desired length. Work 6 rnds of garter st, starting with a purl rnd. Bind off in purl.

Finishing
Attach yarn to side of one row at center back. With crochet hook, work rvs sc around, working 3 sts for every 4 rows. Attach yarn to side of one st at center bottom of each sleeve. With crochet hook, work rvs sc in every st around.

Variation: Bee Stitch Shell
Materials
5 (6, 6) skeins

Bee Stitch
Row 1: *k1, k1 below, rep from *
Row 2: purl
Row 3: k2, k1 below, *k1, k1 below, rep from *; end k1
Row 4: purl

Directions
Work shell as described in the main pattern, substituting Bee Stitch for Double Moss stitch pattern for the yoke.

Variation: Eyelet Shell
Materials
5 (6, 6) skeins

Eyelet Stitch
Row 1: *k2, yo, k2tog, rep from *; end k2
Row 2: purl
Row 3: knit
Row 4: purl
Row 5: k2tog, *k2, yo, k2tog, rep from *; end k2

Row 6: purl
Row 7: knit
Row 8: purl

Directions

Work shell as described in the main pattern, substituting Eyelet Stitch for Double Moss stitch pattern for the yoke.

Variation: Diagonal Rib Shell
Directions

Work shell as described in the main pattern, substituting st st for Double Moss stitch pattern for the yoke.

Body

Pm where each underarm is joined. Join yarn at left side and pick up 94 (100, 108) sts between markers (about 4 sts for every 5 rows). Repeat for the back (188, 200, 216 sts). Be sure to pick up one st in each "corner" at the underarm, between the front and back.

Knit one rnd. Work Rnds 1-14 of Diagnonal Rib, then work Rows 7 to 14 until body is 1¼" shorter than desired length. Work 6 rnds of garter st, starting with a purl rnd. Bind off in purl. Finish as described in the main pattern.

Diagonal Rib

Rnd 1: k2, k2tog, k2, p1, *k3, p1, rep from * to 4 sts before next marker, ssk, k2 Repeat for back of sweater.
Rnd 2: k5, p1, *k3, p1, rep from * around
Rnd 3: k2, k2tog, p1, *k3, p1, rep from * to 4 sts before next marker, ssk, k2 Repeat for back of sweater.
Rnd 4: k3, p1, *k3, p1, rep from * around; end k1
Rnd 5: k2, k2tog, k2, p1, *k3, p1, rep from * to 4 sts before next marker, ssk, k2 Repeat for back of sweater.
Rnd 6: k5, p1, *k3, p1, rep from * around; end k2
Rnd 7 and 8: *p1, k3, rep from * around
Rnd 9 and 10: *k3, p1, rep from * around
Rnd 11 and 12: k2, p1, *k3, p1, rep from * around; end k1
Rnd 13 and 14: k1, p1, *k3, p1, rep from * around, end k2

Variation: Purl-Studded Shell
Directions

Work shell as described in the main pattern, substituting st st for Double Moss stitch pattern for the yoke.

Body

Pm where each underarm is joined. Join yarn at left side and pick up 94 (100, 108) sts between markers (about 4 sts for every 5 rows). Rep for the back (188, 200, 216 sts). Be sure to pick up one st in each "corner" at the underarm, between the front and back.

Knit one rnd. Work Rnd 1-9 of the Dotted Purl pattern, then repeat Rnds 6 to 9 until the body is 1¼" shorter than desired length. Work 6 rnds of garter st, starting with a purl rnd. Bind off in purl. Finish as described in the main pattern.

Dotted Purl

Rnd 1: k2, k2tog, k2, *k3, p1, rep from * to 4 sts before next marker, ssk, k2 Repeat for back of sweater.
Rnd 2: knit
Rnd 3: k2, k2tog, knit to 4 sts before next marker, ssk, k2 Repeat for back of sweater.
Rnd 4: knit
Rnd 5: k2, k2tog, k1, p1, *k3, p1, rep from * to 4 sts before next marker, ssk, k2 Repeat for back of sweater.
Rnds 6, 7, 8: knit
Rnd 9: *p1, k3, rep from *

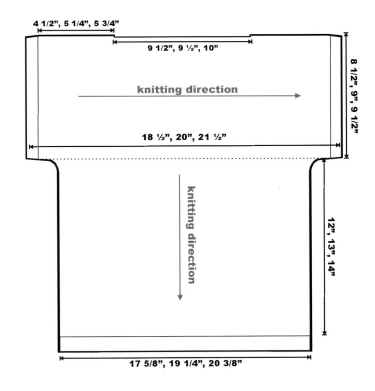

4 1/2", 5 1/4", 5 3/4"

9 1/2", 9 ½", 10"

8 1/2", 9", 9 1/2"

knitting direction

18 ½", 20", 21 ½"

knitting direction

12", 13", 14"

17 5/8", 19 1/4", 20 3/8"

Top Down Raglans

design by Mary Lou Egan

Finished Chest Sizes

S (M, L, XL) measures 40 (44, 48, 50)"

Gauge

20 sts x 28rnds = 4" worked in st st on larger ndl

Materials

5 (6, 7, 7) skeins
US 4 (3.5 mm) 16" and 24" circ ndls
US 7 (4.5 mm) 16" and 24" circ ndl (or size needed to obtain gauge)
Set of US 4 dpns
Set of US 7 dpns

Pattern 145

Note: For m1 (make 1), use a yo increase for a nice, relaxed raglan line. A yo increase also works well because it's easy to see if you are on the increase row or on the plain row. For a symmetrical appearance, use m1-l and m1-r on either side of the raglan stitch.

Directions

Neck

CO 56 (58, 64, 64) sts with larger 24" circ ndl. Work foundation row as follows: p1, pm, p1, pm, p12, pm, p1, pm, p26 (28, 34, 34), pm, p1, pm, p12, pm, p1, pm, p1. **Note:** the sts between the markers are the raglan line sts. Be sure these sts remain between the markers, and the increases are outside of the markers.

Row 1 (RS): Knit in the front and back of the first st, *knit to marked stitch, m1, k1, m1; rep from *; knit in front and back of last st

Row 2: Purl

Rep these two rows until 21 rows are worked, or until center back of neck measures 3". End on a RS row. CO 6 (8, 14, 16) sts for the center front neck, or the number of sts required to make the number of front and back sts equal.

From this point on, the sweater will be knit in the rnd. Join, being careful not to twist; pm for beginning of rnd. If stripes are desired, begin stripes at marker #3.

Rnd 1: knit

Rnd 2: *knit to marked st, m1, knit marked st, m1*; rep from*

Repeat these two rnds 70 (74, 78, 80) more times (352, 372, 400, 412 sts).

Dividing round: knit across the left sleeve sts and the back sts, removing the markers as you come to them. Place the first marked st (beginning of right sleeve), sleeve sts, and next marked st on a length of yarn. CO 4 (8, 8, 8) sts for underarm. Knit across 96 (102, 112, 116) front sts. Put next marked st, 80 (84, 88, 90) sleeve sts, and next marked st on a length of yarn.

Body

CO 4 (8, 8, 8) sts at beginning of rnd for underarm. Join work; pm in the middle of the cast-on sts (200, 220, 240, 248 total sts). Work even until body measures 14 (14½, 15, 15½)" from underarm, or 2" short of desired length. Switch to smaller circ ndl and work edging of choice. For a rolled edge, knit around for 2", bind off loosely. For a hemmed edge, knit to desired length, purl one round for fold line, knit 10 rnds, bind off loosely, and sew hem in place.

Sleeves

With the larger 16" ndl and RS facing, beginning at center of underarm on body, pick up and knit 2 (4, 4, 4) sts. Pick up and twist the strand at the corner where the sleeve meets the body and knit it. Put sleeve sts onto needle and knit them. Pick up and twist the strand at the corner where the sleeve meets the body and knit it. Pick up and knit 2 (4, 4, 4) sts from body. Pm for beg of rnd. First rnd only: slip marker, knit 2 (4, 4, 4), k2tog, Knit until 3 (5, 5, 5) sts before marker, ssk, k1 (3, 3, 3). (This decreases the extra sts picked up at each joining edge of underarm and body).

Knit 5 rounds even. Work a decrease rnd as follows: slip marker, knit first st after marker, k2tog, knit around, ssk before the marker. Knit 5 more rounds. Continue, working a decrease round every sixth rnd, 16 more times (56, 64, 68, 70 sts). Work even until sleeve is 15 (15½, 15½, 16)" from underarm, or 2" short of desired length. Change to dpns when sts no longer fit comfortably on the circ ndl.

To work cuff, dec 14 (18, 20, 22) sts evenly around (42, 46, 48, 48 sts). Change to smaller dpns. For a rolled cuff, knit around for 2". Bind off loosely. Work a second sleeve on the other set of sleeve sts.

Neckband

Using the smaller 16" circ ndl, pick up and knit 96 (102, 112, 116) sts around neck. For a rolled neck, knit around on all sts for 2". Bind-off loosely.

Variation: Ribbed-edge Raglan Directions

Work top down raglan as described in the main pattern. For a ribbed neck, work k1, p1 rib for 1". Bind-off loosely in rib. For ribbed cuffs, work k1, p1 rib for 2". Bind off loosely in rib.

Variation: Positive-Negative Colorwork Gauge

Note: your gauge will probably tighten to 5.25 sts = 1" or more when working in 2-color knitting. To maintain the 5 sts = 1" gauge, use a ndl one size larger.

Materials
4(5, 6, 6) skeins #7809 (Dk. Hyacinth;C1)
3 (3, 4, 4) skeins #8887 (Dk. Lavender; C2)

Directions
Using C1, work top down raglan through the dividing rnd as described in the main pattern. After the dividing rnd, work the body as follows: CO 8 (10, 8, 12) sts at beg of rnd for underarm. Join work; pm in the middle of the cast-on sts (208, 224, 240, 256 sts). Work one rnd in C1. Work Chart A, beginning at the bottom of the chart. After the last row, switch to C2 and work until the body measures 14 (14½, 15, 15½)" from underarm, or 2" short of desired length. Switch to smaller circ ndl and work edging of choice. Finish with a rolled edge or hem. Work sleeves as described in the main pattern.

Hybrid neck
With C1, work k1, p1 ribbing for 4 rnds. With C2, knit 4 rnds. Bind-off loosely.

Variation: Split-Neck Hoodie

Material
7 (7, 8, 8) skeins #9457 (Cobalt Heather)

Directions
Neck
CO 56 (58, 64, 64) sts with larger 24" circ ndl. Work foundation row as follows: p1, pm, p1, pm, p12, pm, p1, pm, p26 (28, 34, 34), pm, p1, pm, p12, pm, p1, pm, p1.
Note: the sts between the markers are the raglan line sts. Be sure these sts remain between the markers, and the increases are outside of the markers.
Row 1 (RS): Knit in the front and back of the first st, *knit to marked stitch, m1, k1, m1; rep from *; knit in front and back of last st
Row 2: Purl
Rep these two rows until 21 rows are worked, or until center back of neck measures 3". End on a RS row.

Placket
At this point, stop increasing at the beginning and end of the row.
Row 1: Knit
Row 2: *Knit to marked st, m1, knit marked st, m1*; rep from*
Rep these two rows 10 more times (20 rows)

At the end of the next RS row, cast on 5 sts. From this point on, the sweater will be knit in the round. Join, being careful not to twist the circle; pm for beg of rnd.
Rnd 1: knit
Rnd 2: *knit to marked st, m1, knit marked st, m1*; rep from*
Rep these 2 rnds 50 (54, 58, 60) more times (352, 372, 400, 412 sts).

Dividing rnd: knit across the left sleeve sts and the back sts, removing markers as you come to them. Place the first marked st (beginning of right sleeve), sleeve sts, and next marked st on a length of yarn. Cast on 4 (8, 8, 8) sts for underarm. Knit across 96 (102, 112, 116) front sts. Put next marked st, 80 (84, 88, 90) sleeve sts, and next marked st on a length of yarn.

Continue working the body and sleeves as described in the main pattern.

Neckband and Hood
With smaller ndl, pick up and knit 76 (80, 80, 84) sts around neck. Work k2, p2 rib for 14 rows. Change to larger ndl, knit 38 (40, 40, 42) sts, pm, finish row.

On next RS row, knit to 2 sts before the marker, m1, k2, m1, work to end of row. Continue to work this increase every knit row 5 (6, 6, 7) times. Work even in st st until hood measures 11 (12, 12, 13)" from rib. To shape hood at center back, knit to 2 sts before the marker, ssk, k2, k2tog. Work this decrease every knit row 5 (6, 6, 7) times total. Weave top of hood together with kitchener stitch.

Finishing
With smaller ndl, beginning one row below cast-on at center neck, pick up 2 sts for every 3 rows along edge of placket and hood. Work 4 rows of st st, purl 1 row (RS), purl 1 row, knit 1 row, purl 1 row, bind off in purl (RS). Sew down. Sew a toggle or a clasp at the neck.

Pocket
CO 30 sts with larger ndl. Work 5 rows st st. Purl 2 rows. Work even in st st for 8" from purl row. Purl two rows, knit 1 row, purl 1 row, knit 1 row, purl 1 row. Bind off. Fold edges at purl fold line, sew down. Pin pocket in place and graft to the front of the sweater in the desired location

---

Variation: Raglan with Staghorn Cable Sleeves

Materials
6 (7, 8, 8) skeins #8229 (Country Green)

Directions
Neck
CO and work the foundation row as described in the main pattern. Set up for cable panel on sleeve as follows:

Row 1 (RS): Knit in the front and back of the first st, *knit to marked st, m1, knit the marked st, *For the sleeve section,* slip marker, M1, place another marker, knit in front and back of sts, k2 (m1, k1) 6 times; end k2, knit in front and back of sts, place another marker, m1 (20 sts in between markers for sleeve section).

In the back section, knit the marked st, m1, knit to marked st, m1, knit the marked st *For the sleeve section,* slip marker, M1, place another marker, knit in front and back of sts, k2 (m1, k1) 6 times; end k2, knit in front and back of sts, place another marker, m1 (20 sts in between markers for sleeve section).
Row 2 (WS): Purl back, keeping the first two and last two sts of sleeve section in garter st (see Chart B).

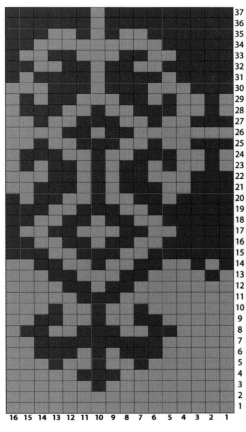

Chart A

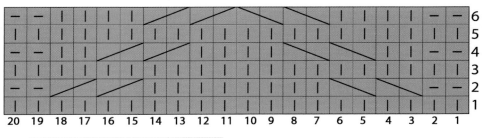

Row 1 (RS): Knit in the front and back of the first st, *knit to marked stitch, m1, k1, m1; rep from *; inserting the cable panel between the two markers in the sleeve sections, knit in front and back of last st.
Row 2 (WS): Purl back, keeping the first two and last two sts of sleeve section in garter st (see Chart B).

Repeat these two rows until there have been 21 rows worked in all, and length measures 3" at center back neck.

From this point on, the sweater will be knit in the rnd. Join, being careful not to twist; pm for beginning of rnd (see Chart B).
Rnd 1: knit, keeping the first two and last two sts of sleeve section in garter st
Rnd 2: *knit to marked st, m1, knit marked st, m1*; rep from*, continuing to work cable panel in sleeve sts.
Repeat these two rnds 70 (74, 78, 80) more times (352, 372, 400, 412 sts, plus 16 sts for cable panel).

Dividing rnd: knit across the left sleeve sts and the back sts, removing the markers as you come to them. Place the first marked st (beginning of right sleeve), sleeve sts, and next marked st on a length of yarn. CO 4 (8, 8, 8) sts for underarm. Knit across 96 (102, 112, 116) front sts. Put next marked st, 80 (84, 88,

Chart B

90) sleeve sts, and next marked st on a length of yarn.

Work the dividing rnd and the body of the sweater as described in the main pattern.

Sleeves
Pick up the sleeve sts as described in the main pattern. There will be 8 more sleeve sts than in the basic pattern. Continue to follow the Chart B. To work cuff, dec 14 (18, 20, 22) sts evenly around, then dec 8

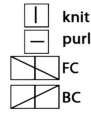

I	knit
—	purl
◺	FC
◹	BC

sts across the last row of the cable panel. Change to smaller dpns. For a rolled cuff, knit around on all sts for 2". Bind off loosely.

Cable Neckband
CO 21 sts. Work Chart B, but insert 1 st in the middle of the panel. Slip this st every RS row. Work for 20, 21, 22, 23 ". Fold piece in half vertically along slipped st. Sew into place around neckline, beginning at left shoulder back; sew folded edge down. Sew seam.

Tomten Hats

design by Ellizabeth Wellenstein

Finished size
One size fits most

Gauge
5.5 sts x 7 rnds= 1" knit in st st the rnd on larger ndl

Materials
1 skein #9404 (Ruby)
US size 3 16" circ ndl
US size 5, 16" circ ndl, or size to obtain gauge
Set of US 5 dpns, or size to match larger circ ndl.

Double dec (dd) = slip next 2 sts knitwise together onto right ndl, k third st, pass 2 sl sts over knit st.

Directions
Brim
With smaller ndl, CO 120 sts. Join work, being careful not to twist the first rnd. Work 5 rnds in rev st st. Change to larger ndls and work 2" in st st. Change back to smaller ndls and work 6 rnds in rev st st.

Pattern 151

Body

Turn work from the RS to the WS and start working in st st. This will be the RS of the body of the hat. There will be a little "blip" in the fabric, but it will be hidden under the brim. Work 1 rnd, then change to larger ndls. Dec 4 sts evenly in next rnd (116 sts).

Work in st st for 4" from bottom rolled edge. Work a dec rnd as follows: *k 26, dd; rep from * to end of rnd (108 sts). Work 2" in st st. Work dec rnd: *k 24, dd; rep from * (100 sts). Work 2" in st st. Work dec rnd: *k 22, dd; rep from * (92 sts). Work 1" in st st. Work dec rnd: *k 20, dd; rep from * (84 sts). Now continue decreasing every alternate rnd in this way until 8 sts rem. Cut tail, thread through rem sts, pull through center to inside, and secure. Weave in ends and attach tassle to top.

Variation: Tomten Hat with 2-Color Brim
Materials
1 skein #9404 (Ruby; MC)
½ skein #8010 (Natural; CC)

Directions
With MC and smaller ndl, CO as in main pattern and work through first 5 rnds of rev st st. Change to larger ndls, work 1 rnd of st st in CC. Pm and work Rnd 1-4 of Chart A. Work Chart B, then Chart A again. Knit 1 rnd in MC and work 6 rnds in rev st st. Work the body of the hat as described in the main pattern.

Variation: Tomten Hat with Cable Brim
Materials
1 skein
cable ndl
US 6 (4.0 mm) 16" circ ndl

C2F (Cross 2 Front): knit into the front of the second st on the ndl, then knit first st, slipping both off the ndl at the same time.
C2B (Cross 2 Back): knit into the back of the second st on the ndl, then knit first st, slipping both off the ndl at the same time.

C4F (Cable 4 Front): slip next 2 sts onto a cable ndl and hold in front, knit 2 sts from LHN, then knit sts from cable ndl.
C4B (Cable 4 Back): slip next 2 sts onto a cable ndl and hold in back, knit 2 sts from LHN, then knit sts from cable ndl.

Directions
CO 120 sts. Pm and join work, being careful not to twist the first rnd. Work cable as follows:
Rnd 1: *p1, k2, p1, k8; rep from *
Rnd 2: *p1, c2b, p1, k8; rep from *
Rnd 3: *p1, k2, p1, c4b, c4f; rep from *
Rnd 4: * p1, c2b, p1, k8; rep from *
Continue working Rnds 1-4 until brim measures 3" from cast-on edge. Purl one rnd. Work the body of the hat as described in the main pattern.

Chart C

Variation: Basketweave Tomten
Materials
1 skein #9429 (Mossy Rock)
Directions
CO 120 sts. Pm and join work, being careful not to twist the first rnd. Work brim as follows:
Rnd 1: knit
Rnd 2: *k1, p3; rep from *
Rnds 3 and 4: rep Rnds 1 and 2
Rnd 5: knit
Rnd 6: * p2, k1, p1; rep from *
Rnds 7 and 8: rep Rnds 5 and 6

Work pattern for approx 3", finishing either on Rnd 4 or Rnd 8. Purl one rnd. Work the body of the hat as described in the main pattern.

Variation: Snowflake Sampler
Materials
1 skein #8010 (Natural; C1)
1 skein #8555 (Black; C2)

Directions
With smaller circ ndl, CO 120. Pm and join work, being careful not to twist the first rnd. Work 6 rnds in st st. Purl one rnd. Change to larger ndl and work 2 rnds in st st. Work Chart C.

Note on decreasing: The decreases are worked with the 2 background sts to the immediate right and left of the vertical bands. On the left side of the band, work a k2tog and on the right, a ssk.

Upon completion of Chart C, adjust sts if necessary so that you have 3 band sts and 3 background sts on each ndl. Work a double dec with band sts, then with background sts for one rnd. Knit 1 rnd on 8 rem sts and finish hat as described in the main pattern. Fold the hem at the purl ridge, whipstitch hem in place, and attach a tassle.

Chart A

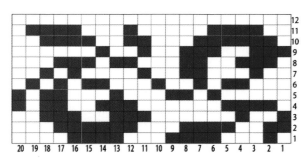

Chart B

61

Womens Vest
design by Urban Tribal Wear Designs

Finished sizes
Chest measurements 32 (36, 40, 44)"

Gauge
5.5 sts x 7 rows = 1" worked in st st on larger ndl

Materials
5 (6, 6, 7) skeins
US 7 (4.5 mm) ndl (or size to obtain gauge)
US 6 (4.0 mm) circ ndl

Directions
Back
CO 88 (100, 112, 124) sts with smaller ndl. Work in k2, p2 rib for 3".
Change to larger ndl and continue in rib until the piece measures 6". Work
in st st until piece measures 12 (12½, 13, 13½)". To shape armholes, bind
off 4 (6, 8, 9) sts at the beg of the next 2 rows, then dec 2 sts on each side
on every RS row 3 (5, 7, 9) times. Work even until the piece measures 20
(21, 22, 23)".

Shape shoulders and back neck:
Bind off 7 (7, 8, 8) sts at the beg of the next row. On the next row, bind off
7 (7, 8, 8) sts, work 13 (14, 15, 16) sts, attach a second ball of yarn, and
bind off 34 (34, 36, 40) sts for the back of the neck. Complete the row.
Working both sides at once, bind off 6 (7, 7, 8) sts and dec 1 st at each
neck edge. Bind off 6 (7, 7, 8) at beg of next row. Bind off 6 (7, 7, 7) sts at
beg of next 2 rows.

Front
Work in two pieces, a right and a left
piece. CO 44 (49, 56, 62) sts with smaller
ndl. Work as for the back, including
armhole shaping. When the piece
measures 19 (20, 21, 21½)", begin the
neck shaping as follows: bind off 12 (12,
13, 13) sts at neck edge, then dec 1 st
every RS row at neck edge 6 (6, 6, 8)
times. Work even until the pieces
measure 20 (21, 22, 23)". Shape the
shoulders to correspond with the back.

Finishing
Sew front and back tog at shoulder and
side seams
With smaller ndl and RS facing, pick up
and knit 112 (116, 122, 124) sts along the
front edge of each piece. Work in k1, p1
rib for 1". Bind off in rib. To work neck
edge, pick up and knit 12 (12, 13, 13) sts
from right front, 12 (15, 13, 19) sts from
side neck, 42 (42, 44, 48) sts from back
neck, 12 (15, 13, 19) from side neck, and
12 (12, 13, 13) left front sts. Work 1" in
k1, p1 rib. Bind off neatly in rib.

With RS facing, pick up and knit 88 (94,
100, 104) sts around armhole. Pm and
join. Work in k1, p1 rib for ¾" . Bind off in
rib.

Pattern 153

**Variation: Fair Isle Vest with Brooch
Closure**

Materials
1 skein each: #7919 (Jade; C1), #8914
(Granny Smith; C2), #2401 (Burgandy;
C3), #7823 (Gold; C4), #8887 (Italian
Plum; C5)

Directions
Back and Front
CO with C5 and work rib in C5 as
described in the main pattern. Then work
Chart A until the pieces measure 12
(12½, 13,13½)". Shape armholes, back
neck, and front neck as described in the
main pattern.

Finishing
With C5, work front edge, neck edge and
armholes as described in the main
pattern.

**Variation: Vest with Cross-over Front
Materials**
3 skeins #9453 (Amethyst Heather; MC)
2 skeins #9441 (Mauve Heather; CC)

Directions
Back
With MC, work as described in the main
pattern, but substituting a 1" border of
seed stitch for the rib.

Right front
CO 44 (49, 56, 62) sts with smaller ndl
and MC. Work 1" of seed stitch. Change
to larger ndl and work in st st as
described in the main pattern.

Left front (cross-over piece)
CO 66 (79, 96,112) sts with smaller ndl
and MC. Work 1" of seed stitch. Work
in st st as for back, including all shaping,
and working the first 6 center edge sts in
seed stitch. When the piece measures 19
(20, 21, 21½)", begin the neck shaping.
Bind off 32 (42, 53, 63) sts at the neck
edge, then dec 1 st at the neck edge
every RS row 6 (6, 6, 8) times. Work even
until the piece measures 20 (21, 22, 23)".
With MC and smaller ndl, pick up and
work 112 (116, 122, 124) sts along
standard front edge in seed stitch. Bind
off in seed stitch.

Neck finishing

Using CC and smaller ndl, with RS facing, pick up and knit 24 (27, 27, 32) sts from the right front neck, 42 (42, 44, 48) sts from the back neck, and 44 (57, 66, 82) sts from the left front neck. Work 6" in k1, p1 rib. Bind off neatly in rib.

Overlap the front of the vest and pin in place with a cool pin, or sew a button on the upper shoulder and crochet a button loop on the top left corner of the vest.

Variation: Ribbed Vest
Materials
3 skeins #8908 (Anis; MC)
2 skeins #8903 (Primaverra; CC)

Directions
CO in CC and work in k2, p2 ribbing for 6". Work remainder of body in st st in MC. Work sleeve finishing in MC, and neck finishing in CC.

Alternatively, work all pieces completely in k2, p2 rib for a figure-hugging look.

Variation: Hooded Vest
Materials
5 skeins #5016

Directions
Work vest front and back as described in the main pattern.

Hood
With larger ndl and RS facing, pick up and knit 21 (22, 22, 26) right front neck sts, 18 (18, 19, 21) of the back sts, pm, 18 (18, 19, 21) remaining back sts, and 21 (22, 22, 26) left front neck sts. Turn. Work in WS row in st st. On next RS row, work first 6 sts in seed stitch, work st st to the last 6 sts, work last 6 sts in seed st. Continue for 2 (2, 2, 2½)". Inc 1 st on each side of the center back marker every 3 (3, 3, 4) rows 22 (18, 14, 5) times, then every 4 (4, 4, 5) rows 1 (4, 7, 10) times. Bind off when the piece measures 12 (12, 12, 12½)". Sew or graft the top together.

Variation: Textured Vest
Materials
5 skeins #8910 (Citron)

Directions
Work vest as described in the Fair Isle pattern, substituting Chart B for Chart A.

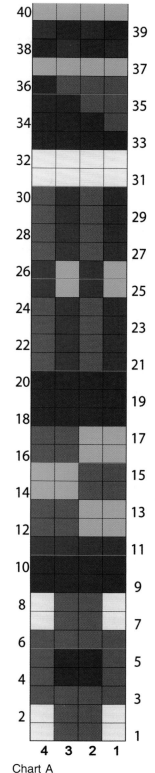

Chart A

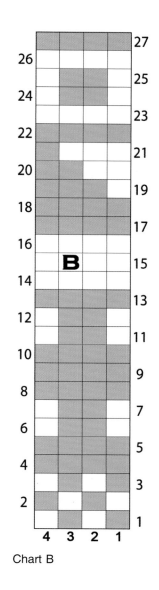

Chart B

	knit on right side, purl on wrong side
	purl on right side, knit on wrong side
B	make bobble

Kids Top Down Raglans

design by Mary Lou Egan

Finished chest sizes
25 (27, 28, 30, 32, 34)"

Gauge
20 sts x 28 rnds = 4" worked in st st on larger ndl

Materials
3 (4, 4, 5, 5, 6) skeins, #_____
US 4 (3.5 mm) 16" and 24" circ ndl
US 7 (4.5 mm) 16" and 24" circ ndl (or size needed to obtain gauge)
Set of US 4 and 7 dpns

Note: For m1 (make 1), use a yo increase for a nice, relaxed raglan line. If your increases are too tight, it will affect your row gauge. This increase is easy to see if you are on the increase row or the plain row. For a symmetrical appearance, use m1-l and m1-r on either side of the raglan stitch.

Directions
Neck
With larger 24" circ ndl, CO 42 (46, 46, 52, 52, 54) sts. Work the foundation row:
p1, pm, p1, pm, p8 (10, 10, 12, 12, 12), pm, p1, pm, p20 (20, 20, 22, 22, 24) (these sts are the neck back), pm, p1, pm (use a different color marker for this third one), p8 (10, 10, 12, 12, 12), pm, p1, pm, p1.
Note: The sts between the markers are the raglan line sts. As subsequent rows are worked, make sure this st keeps its place between the markers, and the increases are outside of the markers.

Row 1 (RS): knit in the front and back of the first st, *knit to marked st, m1, knit the marked st, m1*, rep from * to * until last st, knit in front and back of last st.
Row 2: purl
Rep these two rows until 14 rows are worked, or until length measures 2" at center back of neck.

Center front neck stitches
At the end of the next RS row, CO 6 (6, 6, 8, 8, 10) sts all at once. Note: Before casting on front neck sts, count the front sts (before the first and after the last marker), and the back sts (between the second and third markers). CO 6 (6, 6, 8, 8, 10) sts, or the number of sts needed to make the number of front and back sts equal. Pm and join, being careful not to twist the circle.
Rnd 1: knit
Rnd 2: *knit to marked st, m1, knit marked st, m1*; rep from *

Pattern 160

Repeat these two rnds 13 (18, 22, 26, 30, 35) more times (212, 232, 248, 264, 280, 300 sts).

Dividing rnd: knit across the left sleeve sts and the back sts. **Note:** remove markers as you come to them. Place first marked st (beginning of right sleeve), sleeve sts, and next marked st on a length of yarn. CO 3 sts for underarm. Knit across 60 (64, 68, 72, 76, 82) front sts. Put next marked st, 44 (50, 54, 58, 62, 66) sleeve sts, and next marked st on a length of yarn.

Body
Cast on 3 (3, 3, 3, 4, 3) sts at beg of rnd for underarm. Join work. Pm in middle of cast-on sts. Knit around on 126 (134, 142, 150, 160, 170) body sts. Work even until body is 8 (9, 10, 11, 12, 12)" from underarm, or 2" short of desired length. Switch to smaller circ ndl. For a rolled edge, knit around for 2", bind off loosely.

Sleeves
With larger 16" circ ndl and RS facing, beginning at the center of underarm on body, pick up and knit 1 (1, 1, 1, 2, 1) sts. Pick up and twist the strand at the corner where the sleeve meets the body and knit it. Put 46 (52, 56, 60, 64, 68) sleeve sts

onto ndl and knit them. Pick up and twist the corner st where the sleeve meets the body and knit it. Pick up 2 sts from body. Pm for beg of rnd. First rnd only: slip marker, knit 1 (1, 1, 1, 2, 1), k2tog, knit until 3 sts before marker, ssk, k1.

Knit 5 rnds even. Dec rnd: slip marker, knit first st after marker, k2tog, knit until 2 sts before marker, ssk. Knit 6 (5, 5, 5, 5, 5) more rnds. Continue, working a decrease rnd every fifth round, 4 (7, 8, 10, 11, 12) more times (42, 42, 44, 44, 46, 48 sts). Work even until sleeve is 4½ (6½, 8, 9½, 10½, 11)" from underarm, or 2" short of desired length. Change to dpns when sts no longer fit comfortably on the ndl.

Dec 10 sts evenly around for cuff (32, 32, 34, 34, 36, 38 sts). Change to smaller dpns. For a rolled cuff, knit for 2". Bind off loosely. Work a second sleeve on the other set of sleeve sts.

Neckband
With smaller 16" circ ndl, pick up and knit 70 (70, 74, 80, 80, 84) sts around neck. For a rolled neck, knit for 2". Bind off loosely.

Variation: Striped Raglan
Each stripe is 2 inches, making measuring simple

Materials
Size 2 to Size 7: 1 skein of #8895(Christmas Red; C1), #7814 (Chartreuse; C2), #4147 (Lemon Yellow; C3), #9327 (Dark Colonial Blue Heather; C4)
Size 8 to Size 12: 2 skeins of each color

Directions
CO with C2. Work raglan sweater as described in the main pattern. Every color should be worked for 14 rnds in the following sequence: C1, C2, C3, C4. Use different color markers at the raglan line for changing stripe color later. Switch colors for stripes at marker #3. Remember to change colors in sequence every 14 rounds as you work the sleeves.

Garter edge for body
With the next color in sequence, knit one rnd, purl one rnd. Rep this for each of the other colors. Using the first color of this series of ridges, knit one rnd, then bind off loosely in purl.

Garter edge for cuff
With the next color in sequence, knit one round, purl one round. Rep this for each of the other colors. Using the first color of this series of ridges, knit one rnd, then bind off loosely in purl.

Neckband
With C4 and smaller 16" circ ndl, pick up and knit 70 (70, 74, 80, 80, 84) sts around neck. Knit one rnd, purl one rnd. Switch to C2, knit one rnd, purl one rnd. Switch to C3, knit one rnd, purl one rnd. Switch to C1, knit one rnd, bind off loosely in purl.

Variation: Ruffled Raglan
Materials
Size 2: 1 skein each of #9477(Tutu; C1), #7825 (Orange Sherbet; C2), #8906 (Azur; C3), #9470 (Magenta; C4), #7808 (Purple; C5)
Size 3-6: 2 skeins of #9477(Tutu; C1), 1 skein each of #7825 (Orange Sherbet; C2), #8906 (Azur; C3), #9470 (Magenta; C4), #7808 (Purple; C5)
Size 6-12: 3 skeins of #9477(Tutu; C1), 2 skeins of #7825 (Orange Sherbet; C2), 1 skein each of #8906 (Azur; C3) #9470 (Magenta; C4), #7808 (Purple, C5)

Directions
CO with C1 and work raglan sweater as described in pattern 159. After adding center front neck sts and joining, begin stripes at the third marker, following Chart A until body is 8 (9, 10, 11, 12, 12)"

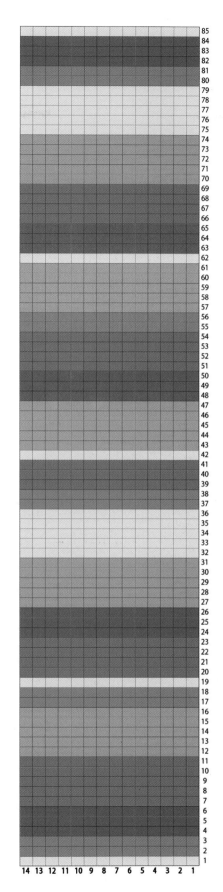

Chart A

from underarm, or 2" short of desired length.

Ruffle
Change color for each rnd, using the same sequence of colors as the body. Twist the new color with the old when changing, carrying up the rnds.

Rnd 1: with next color in sequence, *k2, m1, rep from *
Rnd 2: with next color, knit
Rnd 3: with next color, *k2, m1, rep from *
Rnd 4: with next color, knit
Rnd 5: with next color, *k2, m1, rep from *
Rnd 6: with next color, knit
Rnd 7: with next color, knit
Rnd 8: with next color, *k2, m1, rep from *
Rnd 9: with next color, knit
Rnd 10: with next color, knit
Rnd 11: with next color, knit
Rnd 12: with next color, knit
Rnd 13: with next color, *k1, yo, rep from *
Rnd 14: with next color, bind off all sts loosely, knitting into the yo and not twisting it

Three-quarter sleeves
Work sleeves as described in pattern 159, until sleeve is 3½ (5, 6, 7, 8½, 9)" from underarm. Decrease 6 sts evenly.

Ruffle
Change color for each rnd, using the same sequence of colors as the body. Twist the new color with the old when changing, carrying up the rnds.

Rnd 1: with the next color in sequence, *k2, m1, rep from *
Rnd 2: with next color, knit
Rnd 3: with next color, *k2, m1, rep from *
Rnd 4: with next color, knit
Rnd 5: with next color, knit
Rnd 6: with next color, *k1, yo, rep from *
Rnd 7: with next color, bind off all sts loosely, knitting into the yo and not twisting it

Neckband
Using smaller 16" circ ndl, pick up and knit 65 (65, 70, 75, 75, 80) sts around neck. With C4, knit one rnd. On the next rnd, k1, m1 for entire round. Knit 2 more rnds, bind off loosely.

Northern Star Raglan
Materials
3 (4, 4, 5, 5, 6) skeins #7828 (Bright Yellow)

Directions
Work basic kids raglan as described in the main pattern. After adding the center neck

stitches and joining, pm in the center of the cast-on sts. Work 14 rnds. Place a marker 17 sts on each side of the center marker. Remove the center marker (34 sts between markers). Continue with the basic sweater pattern, working Chart B between these markers.

Body edge
Change to smaller ndl and work k1, p1 rib for 1". Bind-off loosely in rib.

Neckband
Using smaller 16" circ ndl, pick up and knit (70, 74, 80, 80, 84) sts around neck. Work k1, p1 rib for 1". Bind off loosely in rib.

Positive-Negative Colorwork Raglan Gauge
Note: your gauge will probably tighten to 5.25 sts = 1" or more when working in 2-color knitting. To maintain the 5 sts = 1" gauge, use one size larger ndl.

Materials
2 (3, 3, 4, 5)skeins #9444 (Tangerine Heather; MC)
1 (2, 2, 2, 3) skeins #9457 (Cobalt Heather; CC)

Directions
With C1, work the basic kids raglan as described in the main pattern. After the dividing round, CO 3 (5, 4, 3, 4, 4) sts at beginning of round for underarm. Join work, placing a marker in the middle of cast-on sts (126, 138, 144, 150, 162, 174 total body sts). Work one rnd in C1. Work Chart C, beginning at the bottom. When Chart C is complete, continue in C2. Switch to smaller circ ndl and knit around for 2", bind off loosely.

Hybrid neck
With C1 and smaller 16" circ ndl, pick up and knit 70 (70, 74, 80, 80, 84) sts around neck. Work k1, p1 rib for 4 rnds. Change to C2 and knit 4 rnds. Bind off loosely.

☐ knit

• purl

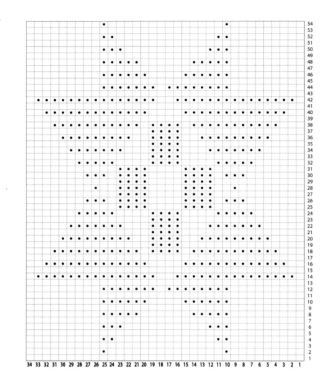

Chart B

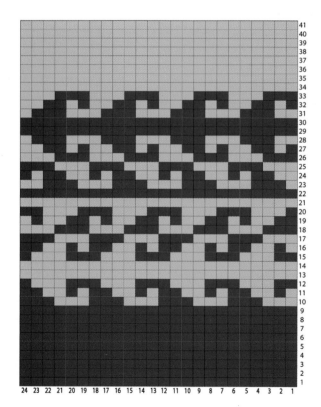

Chart C

Fair Isle Cardigans
design by Urban Tribal Wear Designs

Finished sizes
Chest measurement: 32 (36, 40, 45)"

Gauge
5.5 sts x 7rows = 1" worked in st st on larger ndl

Materials
6(6, 7, 8) skeins total; 1 of each, plus 1 extra of C4:
#8911 (Grape Jelly; C1)
#7815 (Summer Sky; C2)
#9423 (Teal; C3)
#8903 (Primaverra; C4)
#2403 (Chocolate; C5)

Optional colorway
#9459 (Yakima Heather; C1)
#9445 (Autumn Heather; C2)
#9461 (Lime Heather; C3)
#9441 (Mauve Heather; C4)
#9451 (Lake Chelan Heather; C5)

US 7 (4.5 mm) ndl (or size needed to obtain gauge)
US 6 (4.0 mm) 16" circ ndl
1½" pin for the flower pin

Pattern key
B = Make bobble. Knit in the front, back & front of the next st. Turn. P3, turn, k3, turn, p3, turn, sl 1, k2tog, psso. Bobble complete.

Pattern 163

Directions
Back
CO 88 (100, 112, 124) sts with smaller ndl and C4. Work in k2, p2 rib for 4". Change to larger ndl and work Chart A until the piece measures 14 (14½,15, 15½)". To shape armholes, bind off 4 (6, 8, 9) sts at the beg of the next 2 rows. Dec 1 st on each side of every RS row 3 (5, 7, 9) times. Continue to work Chart A until the piece measures 8 (8½, 9, 9½)" from the beginning of the armhole.

Shoulder and back neck shaping
Bind off 7 (7, 8, 8) sts at the beg of the next row. At beg of the next row, bind off 7 (7, 8, 8) sts, work 13 (14, 15, 16) sts, attach a second ball of yarn, and bind off 34 (34, 36, 40) sts for the back neck. Complete row. At the beg of the next row, bind off 6 (7, 7, 8) sts and dec 1 st at each neck edge. Bind off 6 (7, 7, 8) sts at the beg of the next row. Bind off 6 (7, 7, 7) sts at beg of next 2 rows.

Front
Make 2 pieces, reversing the shaping for the second piece. With smaller ndl and C4, CO 44 (50, 56, 62) sts starting with

Stitch 1 (3, 1, 3) on the Chart A. Work as for back, including all shaping and, at the same time, when the piece measures 6 (6½, 7, 7½)" from the armhole bind off, begin the neck shaping. Bind off 12 (12, 13, 13) sts at neck edge, then dec 1 st at neck edge every RS row 6 (6, 6, 8) times. Continue to work Chart A until the pieces measure 8 (8½, 9, 9½)" from armhole bind-off. Shape shoulders to correspond with the back.

Sleeves
CO 46 (50, 52, 58) sts with smaller ndl and C4. Work in k2, p2 rib for 1". Work Chart A until the sleeve measures 7". Change to larger ndl and C5. Working in st st, begin sleeve shaping as follows: inc 1 st on each side of every RS row 17 (19, 23, 21) times, then every 4 rows 4 (3, 1, 2) times. Work even until the sleeve measures 15".

Change to C4 and begin cap shaping. Bind off 4 (6, 8, 9) sts on each side, then dec 1 st on each side of every RS row 3 (5, 7, 9) times. Dec 1 st each side every row 24 (21, 17, 15) times, then every RS row 0 (1, 2, 2) times. Bind off 3 (4, 4, 4)

sts at the beg of the next 4 rows. Bind off rem 14 (16, 16, 18) sts.

Finishing
Sew shoulder and side seams. Sew in sleeves and sleeve seams. Using smaller ndl and C4, with RS facing, pick up 118 (123, 128, 133) sts along front edge, and work in k1, p1 rib for 1". Bind off neatly in rib. Rep for other edge.

For neck, using smaller ndl and with RS facing, pick up 25 (27, 26, 32) right front sts, 42 (42, 44, 48) back neck sts, and 25 (27, 26, 32) left side neck sts. Work back and forth in k1, p1 rib for 1". Bind off loosely in rib.

Flower pin:
CO 50 sts with smaller ndl and C5. Work 4 rows in st st. On the next RS row *k1, m1, rep from * to the end of the row. Work 3 rows in st st. Bind off. Roll the strip into a rose and sew the layers in place along the bottom. Sew a 1½" pin onto the bottom of the flower.

Leaf:
CO 4 sts with C2.
Row 1 (RS): knit
Row 2 and all even rows: purl
Row 3: k2, m1, k2
Row 5: k2, m1, k1, m1, k2
Row 7: k3, m1, k1, m1, k3
Row 9: k4, m1, k1, m1, k4
Row 11: k5, m1, k1, m1, k5
Row 13: 15, 17: knit
Bind off
Gather the bottom of the leaf and stitch to
the bottom of the rose.

Variation: Add a Collar
Directions
Work sweater pieces as described in the
main pattern. With smaller ndl and C4,
with RS facing, pick up 25 (27, 26, 32)
right front sts, 42 (42, 44, 48) back neck
sts, and 25 (27, 26, 32) left side neck sts.
Work back and forth in k1, p1 rib or seed
stitch for 6". Bind off loosely in pattern.

**Variation: Solid Color Sweater with
Full-length Cuffed Sleeve**
Materials
6 (6, 7, 8) skeins C1
1 skein C2

Directions
Work front and back pieces as described
in the main pattern, using a single color.

Sleeves
CO 46 (50, 52, 58) sts with smaller ndl.
Work in k1, p1 rib for 6". Change to larger
ndl and C2. Working in st st, work one RS
row. Shape sleeves as follows: inc 1 st
each side every 4 rows 16 (16, 21,16)
times, then every 6 rows 5 (6, 3,7) times.
Continue in st st until the piece measures
17 (17½, 18, 18½)". Shape cap as
described in the main pattern.

Variation: Add a Lacing Front
Materials
6 (6, 7, 8) skeins
7' of 1"-wide ribbon

Directions
Work the back, fronts, and sleeves of a
Fair Isle or a solid color cardigan as
described in the main pattern. Sew the
pieces together.

Finishing
With smaller ndl and C4, with RS facing,
pick up 118 (123, 128, 133) sts along
front edge. Work in k1, p1 rib for 2 rows.
*Work 6 sts, yo, k2tog, rep from * to end
of row, ending with "work 6". Cont in k1,
p1 rib until the band measures 1". Work

the second band. Lace the ribbon
through the eyelets starting at the top. Tie
a bow at the bottom.

Variation: Purled Twist-Knot Texture
*This is simple pattern with a nubby,
chanel-like texture*

Materials
6 (6, 7, 8) skeins #9441 (Mauve Heather)
Optional: 1 skein #8914 (Granny Smith;
CC)

Purled Twist-Knot
Row 1 and 3 (WS): purl
Row 2: *k2, p2tog and leave on ndl,
insert RHN from the back between the
P2tog sts and purl the first st again, then
sl both sts from ndl tog; rep from *
Row 4: *p2 tog and purl first st again (as
in Row 2), k2, rep from *

Directions
Work sweater as described in the main
pattern, working the body of all pieces in
Purled Twist-Knit pattern stitch. Optional:
work the rib and finishing bands with CC.

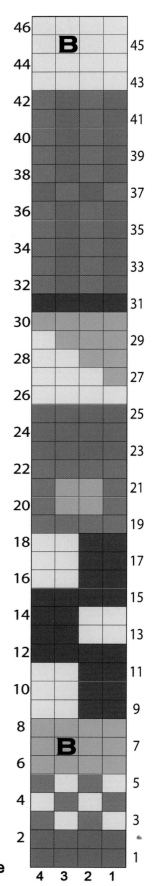

Chart A

☐ knit on right side, purl on wrong side

B make bobble

Shawdow Knit Scarves
design by Patti Pierce Stone

Also known as illusion knitting, shadow knitting is most easily viewed in a more firmly-knit fabric, so work these scarves with needles smaller than you might otherwise use

Finished size
About 60"

Gauge
19 sts x 32 rows = 4" worked in shadow pattern

Notes on shadow knitting: the shadow knitting charts used in these patterns are 2-row charts that indicate the sts on the even-numbered WS rows. All RS (odd-numbered) rows are knit *using the the same color as the following even-numbered row.* For example, Row 1 MC, Row 2 MC, Row 3 CC, Row 4 CC. The chart and legend indicate which stitches are to be knit or purled on the wrong side rows.

All slipped sts should be slipped purlwise with the yarn forward.

Lots of Dots Scarf
Worked end to end with ring fringe

Materials
1 skein #8400 (Charcoal Grey; MC)
1 skein #4192 (Soft Pink; CC)
US 6 (4.25 mm) ndl
8 1" plastic drapery rings
US E crochet hook,

Directions
CO 35 sts with CC, using a long tail cast-on method. Knit 6 rows, slipping last 2 sts. Attach MC and knit one row, slipping the last 2 sts. Beginning with Row 2 (WS), work 7 repeats of the Chart A. Slip the last 2 sts on all odd-numbered rows.

Finishing
After working last row of chart, cut CC . Knit 6 rows plain, slipping the last two sts. Bind off evenly from RS. Cut yarn, leaving a 6" tail. Pull tail through remaining stitch to secure. Weave in ends.

Ring fringe
With crochet hook and CC, single crochet over the drapery rings to cover completely (approx 30 sts per ring). Cover half of the rings with MC, if desired. Alternatively, thread a tapestry needle with a 36" length of CC and use a blanket stitch to cover the rings. Cut yarn, leaving a 12" tail.

To join rings, thread the tail from one ring into a tapestry needle. Take 2 or 3 sts from front to back (the bumpy side, if crocheted) of the center 2 sts on the bottom of another ring. The bottom center will be exactly across from the tail. Weave

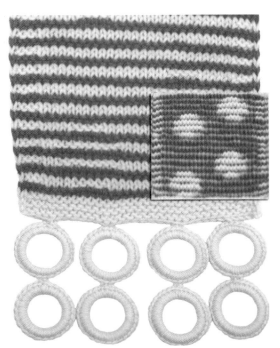

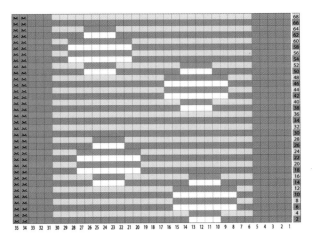

Pattern 168

169

all right side rows: knit to last 2 st, sl 2
wrong side rows, work according to chart

▩	MC - knit
☐	MC - purl
▨	CC - knit
☐	CC - purl
⋊	slip stitch purlwise

Chart A

tail under 3 or 4 sts on the back side of the ring, then cut and secure. Rep 3 times, making four 2-ring groups.

Lay the blocked scarf on a flat surface and position the ring fringe evenly along the bottom of the short edge of the scarf. Mark with a straight pin where the center of each ring touches the scarf. Thread the remaining tail and, as before, join each strand of rings with 2 or 3 sts to the lower edge where marked. Weave tail under 3 or 4 stitches on the back side of the ring and secure. Rep for the other end of the scarf.

Variation: Barber Pole Shadow Scarf
Worked from center to ends

Materials
1 skein #8555 (Black; MC)
1 skein #8505 (White)

Directions
CO 35 with MC, using a provisional cast-on method. Beginning with Row 2 (WS), work 5 repeats of the Chart B. Slip the last 2 sts in all odd-numbered rows.

69

Finishing - Side 1

After working last row of chart, cut CC. With MC, knit 14 rows plain, slipping the last two sts on each row. Bind off loosely from RS. Begin decrease bind-off as follows: k1, *slip just worked st back to nonworking needle, k2tog. Rep from * until one loop remains. Cut yarn, leaving a 6" tail. Pull tail through remaining stitch and secure.

Side 2

With RS facing, remove provisional cast on and place open sts onto ndl. For ease of counting, pm to mark the middle of the scarf. On RS, beginning with row 3 of the Chart B, work 5 repeats of Chart B in reverse (begin at left side of chart and work to right). Slip the last 2 sts on each row, not the first two. Finish as for the first side.

Side-to-Side Shadow Scarf
Worked end to end with tassel fringe

Materials
1 skein #8555 (Black; MC)
1 skein #8884 (Claret; CC)

Directions
CO 35 sts with MC, using a long-tail cast-on method. Knit 5 rows, slipping the last 2 sts. Attach CC and knit one row, slipping the last 2 sts. Beginning with row 2 (WS), work 6 repeats of Chart C, then work rows 2 – 36 again. Slip the last 2 sts on all odd-numbered rows.

Finishing
With CC, knit 2 rows, slipping the 2 sts each row, cut yarn. Knit 5 rows with MC, slipping the last 2 sts. Bind off evenly from RS. Cut yarn, leaving a 6" tail. Pull tail through rem st and secure.

Tasseled fringe
Make and attach 9 tassels as follows: cut 12 5-inch lengths of CC for each tassel. Beginning in the second stitch from the edge of the short end of the scarf, pull all 12 strands halfway through the stitch (easily done with a crochet hook). Fold the strands in half. Using a 6" length of MC, tightly wrap the strands of yarn twice, about ¼" from edge of scarf, then knot. Use a tapestry needle to thread the MC ends individually into the center of the tassel. Trim tassel to about ½" from tie. *Skip 3 st and create next tassel. Rep from * across. The last tassel should be in the second stitch from the end of the row. Make and attach tassels for the other end of the scarf.

Variation: Going-In-Circles Shadow Scarf
Materials
1 skein #9419 (Vermeer Blue; MC)
1 skein #7808 (Purple Hyacinth; CC)

Bobble Border
Row 1 and 3 (MC): k2, p1,*k5, p1, rep from * to last 2 st, sl 2
Row 2 (WS) (MC): k2, p to last 2 sts, sl 2
Row 4: MC k2, p3, [CC p1, MC p5] 4 times.CC p1, MC p3, sl 2
Row 5: MC k2, p1, *MC k2, CC bobble, MC k2, p1, rep from * to last 2 sts, sl 2
Row 6: rep Row 2
Row 7: rep Row 1
Rows 8 and 9: rep row 2

Bobble: knit into back, front, back, front of next st (4 sts created), turn. k4, turn, p4, pass second, third, and fourth st individually over first st and off the ndl. Turn. Bobble complete.

Directions
CO 35 sts with MC, using a long-tail cast-on method. Knit 2 rows, slipping the last 2 sts of each row. Work rows 1-9 of Bobble Border, then work rows 2-9 again. With MC, knit one row, slipping last 2 sts. Beginning with row 2, work Chart D once, slipping the last 2 sts of all odd-numbered rows.

Scarf middle
All RS rows: k2, p1, k to last 3 sts, p1, sl 2
All WS rows: k2, p to last 2 st, sl 2
Work these two rows until this section measures 45" (or scarf measure 8" shorter than desired length).

Pattern 169

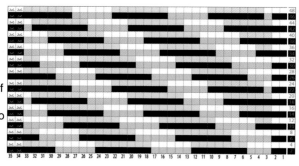

Chart B

all right side rows: knit to last 2 st, sl 2
wrong side rows, work according to chart

■ MC - knit

▨ MC - purl

□ CC - knit

▤ CC - purl

∿ slip stitch purlwise

Work Chart D as before, beginning with row 48 and working backward to row 1. On the next row, k2, p to last 2 st, sl 2. Work rows 1-9 and 2-9 of the Bobble Border as before. On the next row, k2, p to last 2 sts, sl 2. Bind off evenly in purl.

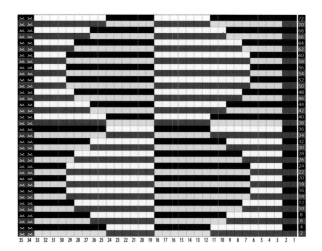

Chart C

all right side rows: knit to last 2 st, sl 2
wrong side rows, work according to chart

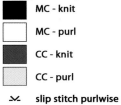

- ■ MC - knit
- □ MC - purl
- ■ CC - knit
- ■ CC - purl
- ⋎ slip stitch purlwise

Pattern 170

Pattern 171

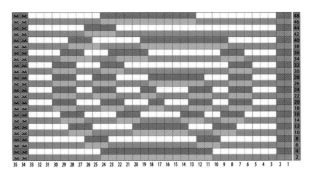

Chart D

all right side rows: knit to last 2 st, sl 2
wrong side rows, work according to chart

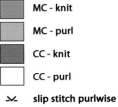

- ■ MC - knit
- ■ MC - purl
- ■ CC - knit
- □ CC - purl
- ⋎ slip stitch purlwise

Cabled Headbands

design by Elizabeth Wellenstein

Finished sizes
Average woman (average man) 21(22)"
Note on size: knit the band 1" shorter
than head measurement

Gauge
approx 6 sts = 1" worked in cable pattern

Materials
1 skein #4010 (Straw)
US 5 (3.75 mm) ndl
Cable ndl

Braided Plait
Row 1 (RS): k1, p2, pm, k27, pm, p2, k1
Note: beg with row 2, with yarn in front, sl
the first st of every row. This creates nice
selvage edges.
Row 2: sl 1, p1, k1, p27, k1, p1, k1
Row 3: sl 1, p2, k3, *c6f, rep from * 3
more times, p2, k1
Row 4: sl 1, p1, k1, p27, k1, p1, k1
Row 5: sl 1, p2, k27, p2, k1
Row 6: sl 1, p1, k1, p27, k1, p1, k1
Row 7: sl 1, p2, *c6b, rep from * 3 more
times, k3, p2, k1
Row 8: sl 1, p1, k1, p27, k1, p1, k1

C6F: sl next 3 sts onto cn and hold in
front of work, knit the next 3 sts from
LHN, then knit sts from cn.
C6B: sl next 3 sts onto cn and hold in
back of work, knit the next 3 sts from the
LHN, then knit sts from cn.

Directions
CO 33 sts and purl 1 row. Work Braided
Plait until piece measures 21 (22)" or
desired length. Before seaming, decrease
approx 1/3 of the sts so that the ends of
the headband don't flare. Work the dec
rows as follows: knit to 3 sts before
marker, k2tog across the cables so that
the 6-st cable becomes 3 sts, then knit
the 3 rem sts that are not crossed (or knit
them first, depending where you stopped
knitting). Knit 3 sts after marker (21 sts).
Bind off in purl. At the cast-on edge, with
RS facing, knit up the same number of
sts, bind off in purl.

Finishing
With RS facing outward, bring edges
together. You should see the 'V's of the
bound-off edges. Whipstitch the adjacent
legs of the 'V's together.

Pattern 173

Variation: Side-by-Side Cable Headband
Materials
1 skein #2414 (Ginger)

4-Stitch Cable
Row 1(RS): k24
Row 2: p24
Row 3: *c4f, rep from * 5 more times
Row 4: p24

C4F: sl next 2 sts onto cn and hold in
front of work, knit the next 2 sts from
LHN, then knit sts from cn.

Directions
CO 30 sts. Work the headband as
described in the main pattern, working
the edge sts, but substituting 4-Stitch
Cable for Braided Plait between the
markers. Work dec rows by k2tog across
each cable so that a 4-st cable becomes
2 sts. You should have 18 sts. Finish as
described in the main pattern.

Variation: 6-Stitch Cable Headband
Materials
1 skein #9338 (Lichen)

6-Stitch Cable
Row 1 (RS): (k2,c4f, p1) 3 times, k2, c4f
Row 2: (p6, K1) 3 times, p6
Row 3: (c4b, k2, p1) 3 times, c4b, k2
Row 4: (p6, k1) 3 times, p6

C4F: sl next 2 sts onto cn and hold in
front of work, knit the next 2 sts from
LHN, then knit sts from cn.

C4B: sl next 2 sts onto cn and hold in
back of work, knit the next 2 sts from the
LHN, then knit sts from cn.

Directions
CO 33 sts. Work the headband as
described in the main pattern, working
the edge sts, but substituting 6-Stitch
Cable for Braided Plait between the
markers. Work dec rows by k2tog across
each cable so that a 4-st cable becomes
2 sts. End with 21 sts. Finish as
described in the main pattern

Variation: Cable and Lattice Headband
Materials
1 skein #9345 (Wisteria)

Cable and Lattice
Row 1(RS): k4, p3, c4b, p4, c4b, p3, k4
Row 2: p4, k3, p4, k4, p4, k3, p4
Row 3: c4b, p1, t4b, t4f, t4b, t4f, p1, c4b
Row 4: p4, k1, p2, k4, p4, k4, p2, k1, p4
Row 5: k4, p1, k2, p4, c4b, p4, k2, p1, k4
Row 6: rep row 4
Row 7: c4b, p1, t4f, t4b, t4f, t4b, p1,c4b
Row 8: rep row 2

T4B=twist 4 back. Sl next 2 sts to cn,
hold at back of work. K next 2 sts from
LHN, purl sts from cn.
T4F=twist 4 front. Sl next 2 sts to cn,
hold at front of work. P next 2 sts from
LHN, knit sts from cn.

Directions
CO 32 sts. Work the headband as
described in the main pattern, working

the edge sts, but substituting Cable and Lattice for Braided Plait between the markers. Work dec rows by k2tog across each cable so that a 4-st cable becomes 2 sts. End with 20 sts. Finish as described in the main pattern

Variation: Wishbone Cable Headband
Materials
1 skein #8401 (Sliver Grey)

Wishbone Cable
Row 1 (RS): c2b, p1, k8, p1, c2b, p1, k8, p1, c2b
Row2: p2, k1, p8, k1, p2, k1, p8, k1, p2

Row3: c2b, p1, c4b, c4f, p1, c2b, p1, c4b, c4f, p1, c2b
Row 4: rep row 2

C2F: sl next st onto cn and hold in front of work, knit the next st from LHN, then knit st from cn.
C2B: sl next st onto cn and hold in back of work, knit the next st from the LHN, then knit st from cn.
C4F: sl next 2 sts onto cn and hold in front of work, knit the next 2 sts from LHN, then knit sts from cn.

Directions
CO 32 sts. Work the headband as described in the main pattern, working the edge sts, but substituting Wishbone Cable for the Braided Plait between the markers. Work dec rows by k2tog across each cable so that a 4-st cable becomes 2 sts, and a 2-st cable becomes 1 st. End with 21 sts. Finish as described in the main pattern.

176

Mens Hooded Pullover
design by Urban Tribal Wear Designs

Finished sizes
Finished chest measurement 40 (44, 48, 52)"

Gauge
5.5 sts x 7rows = 1" worked in st st on larger ndl

Materials
9 (9, 11, 13) skeins #8400 (Charcoal Grey; MC)
1 skein #9428 (Green ; CC)
US 7 (4.5 mm) 24" (40 cm) circ ndl (or size to obtain gauge)
US 6 (4.0 mm) 24" circ ndl
5' suede lacing for hood drawstring

Directions
Back
CO 110 (122, 132,144) sts with smaller ndl and CC. Work 4 rows in k1, p1 rib. Change to MC and continue in k1, p1 rib until the piece measures 3". Change to larger ndl and continue in k1, p1 rib until the piece measures 15½ (16, 17, 17½)".

Shape armholes as follows: bind off 4 (6, 7, 8) sts at beg of next 2 rows, then dec 1 st each side every RS row 4 (5, 7, 8) times. Cont in rib until the piece measures 25, (26½, 28½, 31)". Begin shoulder shaping as follows: bind off 8 (9, 9, 10) sts at beg of next 2 (6, 4, 6) rows. Bind off 9 (0, 10, 0) at beg of next 4 (0, 2, 0) rows, then bind off 42 (46,48, 52) back neck sts.

Front
Work as for back including all shaping and, at the same time, when the piece measures 24 (24, 26, 28)" begin neck shaping as follows: work 36 (37, 39, 42) sts, join second ball of yarn, and bind off center 22 (26, 26, 28) sts. Work the rem 36 (37, 39, 42) sts. Working both sides at once, dec 1 st each neck edge every RS row 10 (11, 12) times. Continue in ribbing until the piece measures 9½ (10½, 11,

13½)" from armhole bind-off. Shape the shoulders to correspond with the back.

Sleeves
CO 56 (60, 66, 70) sts with CC and smaller ndl. Work 4 rows in k1, p1 rib. Change to MC and continue in k1, p1 ribbing until the sleeve measures 6". Change to larger ndl and shape sleeves as follows: inc 1 st each side every 4 (4,

4, 2) rows 17 (26, 30, 14) times, then 1 st every 6 (6, 0, 4) rows 7 (2, 0, 5) times. Continue in rib until the sleeve measures 22½ (23½, 24, 25)".

To shape cap, bind off 4 (6, 7, 8) sts at the beg of the next 2 rows. Dec 1 st each side every RS row 4 (5, 7, 7) times. Dec 1

177

Pattern 177

73

st each side every row 25 (26, 23, 26) times, then every RS row 2 (3, 5, 7) times. Bind off 4 (4, 5, 6) sts at beg of next 4 rows. Bind off rem 18 (20, 22, 26) sts.

Finishing

Sew shoulder and side seams together. Sew in sleeves. Sew sleeve seams.

Drawstring Hood

CO 6 sts with CC (for the hem), pm, and with RS facing, starting on Stitch 12 (13, 14, 14) of the front neck sts, pick up and knit 11(12, 13, 13) front neck sts, 14 (16, 16, 20) side neck sts, 21 (22, 24, 25) back neck sts, pm, pick up and knit the rest of the back neck sts, 14 (16, 16, 20) side neck sts, and 11 (12, 13, 13) front neck sts, pm, CO 6 sts. Working back and forth in st st, work 1 WS row. Work even for 3 (3½, 3½, 3½)". Inc 1 st on each side of center marker every 4 (6, 5, 5) rows 10 (7, 8, 8) times, then every 5 (7, 6, 6) rows 6 (4, 5, 5) times. Bind off when the hood measures 13 (13½, 13½, 13½)". Sew the top, fold hem and slip stitch in place. Run a suede drawstring through the gusset.

Variation: Standard Crew Neck
Materials

9 (9, 11, 13) skeins #2432 (Cameleon; MC)
1 skein #9451 (Lake Chelan Heather)

Directions

Work sweater as described in the main pattern, except for the hood.

Neck finishing

Using the smaller ndl and CC, and with RS facing, pick up and knit 106 (116, 120, 136) sts evenly around the neck edge. Work in k1, p1 rib for 1". Bind off loosely in rib.

Variation: Turtleneck Sweater
Directions

Work sweater as described in the main pattern, except for the hood.

Neck finishing

With smaller ndl and MC, and with RS facing, pick up and knit 106 (116, 120, 136) sts evenly around the neck edge. Work in k1, p1 rib for 5". Change to CC and work in k1, p1 rib until the collar measures 5¼". Bind off loosely in rib

Variation: Striped Sweater
Materials

2 skeins #8013 (Walnut Heather; C1)
2 skeins #8012 (Doeskin Heather; C2)
2 skeins #2439 (Gelato; C3)
2 skeins #4010 (Straw; C4)
2 skeins #9444 (Tangerine Heather; C5)

Directions

Work sweater as described in the main pattern, working stripes in the following order throughout:
Row 1-6: C1
Row 7-8: C2
Row 9-14: C3
Row 15: C4
Row 16-22: C5
Row 23-26: C2
Row 27-35: C4
Row 36: C1
Row 37-40: C3

Variation: Diamond Sweater

9 (9, 11, 13) skeins #4147 (Lemon Yellow; MC)

Directions
Back

CO 110 (122, 132,144) sts with smaller ndl. Work in st st for 3". Change to larger ndl and finish the piece in st st as described in the main pattern.

Front

CO 110 (122, 132,144) sts with smaller ndl. Work in st st for 3". Change to larger ndl and work in st st until the piece measures 8½ (9, 10, 10½)". Work Chart A, starting the pattern at the selected size. Work chart to the center, then work the pattern in reverse.

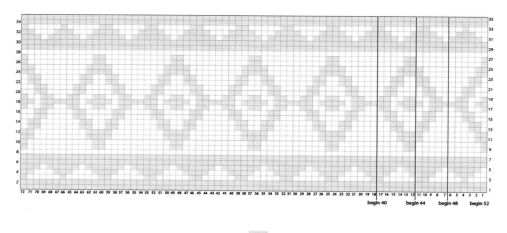

Chart A

knit on right side, purl on wrong side
purl on right side, knit on wrong side

Boot Socks

design by Mary Lou Egan

Finished sizes
Adult M (L, XL)
M generally fits a woman's foot or a narrow man's foot; L fits a wider foot or an average man's foot; XL fits a wide man's foot

Gauge
12 sts = 2"

Materials
2 skeins
Reinforcing yarn for heel and toe (optional)
Set of US 3 (3.25 mm) dpns (or size needed to obtain gauge)

Rib Stitch
Rnd 1: knit
Rnd 2: k1, p1

Directions

Leg
CO 48 (52, 56) sts loosely. A loose cast-on is critical for sock cuffs. If necessary, CO on over two needles held together. Join, being careful not to twist the sts. Divide sts so that the first ndl has 12 (12, 16) sts, the second ndl has 24 (28, 24) sts, and the third needle has 12 (12, 16) sts. Work around in k2, p2 rib for 2". Change to Rib Stitch and work for 6" or desired length to top of ankle bone.

Heel flap
At beg of next rnd, knit 12 (13, 14) sts, turn, sl 1, p23 (25, 27). These 24 (26, 28) sts will be worked back and forth for the heel flap. If reinforcing yarn is desired, begin using it here. Divide rem sts over two ndls.
Row 1: *sl 1, k1*, rep from *
Row 2: sl 1, purl to end
Rep these two rows until 25 rows have been completed, ending with a RS row.

Turn heel
Row 1: p14 (14, 15), p2tog, p1, turn
Row 2: sl 1, k5 (5, 5), k2tog, k1, turn
The turn creates a gap.
Next row: sl 1, p to within 1 st of the gap, p2tog (closing the gap), p1, turn
Next row: sl 1, k to within 1 st of the gap, k2tog, k1, turn
Rep the last two rows until all sts have been used up, and 14 (16, 18) sts remain on ndl.
Break off reinforcing yarn, leaving an end to darn in.

Heel Gusset
With the same ndl, pick up and knit 12 sts along the right side of the heel. Pick up and twist the running thread in the gap between the heel flap and the first instep ndl. Put this st on the ndl with the picked-up heel flap sts. Work across the instep sts, keeping them in the pattern stitch and on one ndl. With an empty ndl, pick up and twist the running thread in the gap between the instep ndl and the heel flap.

With the same ndl, pick up and knit 12 sts along the left side of heel. Knit 7 (8, 9) sts (half of heel) from the first ndl. There should be 20 (21, 21) sts on ndl #1, 24 (26, 28) sts on the instep ndl (#2), and 20 (21, 21) sts on ndl #3. The round now begins in the middle of the heel.
Rnd 1: knit.
Rnd 2: knit to last 3 sts on ndl #1, k2tog, k1. Work pattern stitch across the instep ndl sts. At the beg of needle #3, k1, ssk, knit to end of ndl.
Continue working these two rnds until there are 48 (52, 56) sts remaining, with 12 (13, 14) sts on ndl #1, 24 (26, 28) sts on ndl #2, and 12 (13,14) sts on ndl #3.

Foot
Work as established, with the pattern stitch on the instep ndl (#2), and the other two ndl in st st, until foot is about 1½" shorter than desired length.

Toe
Rnd 1: knit to last 3 sts on ndl #1, k2tog, k1. At the beg of ndl #2, k1, ssk, knit to last 3 sts on ndl, k2tog, k1. At the beg of ndl #3, k1, ssk, knit to end of ndl.
Rnd 2: knit
Rep these two rnds until there are 24 (24, 28) sts remaining. Break yarn, leaving a 12-inch tail. Divide stitches over two needles, 12 (12, 14) sts on each needle. Graft toe together with kitchener stitch.

Variation: Mistake Stitch Rib

Mistake Stitch Rib

Rnd 1: *k2, p2; rep from *
Rnd 2: k1, *p2, k2; rep from *, end p2, k1

Directions
Work k2, p2 rib for 2". Work Mistake Stitch Rib for 8", or desired length to top of ankle bone. Work heel and foot as described in the main pattern, working foot in st st (knit all rnds).

Pattern 184

75

Variation: Slouch Sock
Directions

Work as described in the main pattern, but after 2" of k2, p2 rib, work in st st for 10 rnds, *purl 2 rnds, knit 5 rnds*; rep from * for 8" or desired length to top of ankle bone.. Work heel and foot as described in the main pattern, working foot in st st.

Variation: Irene's Cable Sock
Finished size: M

Cable Pattern
Rnd 1: knit
Rnd 2: knit
Rnd 3: *k5, sl next 2 sts to dpn or cable ndl, hold in back, k2, k2 from dpn, sl next 2 sts to dpn and hold in front, k2, k2 from dpn* repeat from * 3 more times

Directions

CO 48 (52, 56) sts loosely. Work k2, p2 ribbing for 2". Work Cable Pattern for 6" or desired length to top of ankle bone. Work heel and foot as described for size M in the main pattern.

Variation: Slip Stitch Socks
Gauge
Slip stitch tightens gauge, so check gauge carefully to ensure the leg will not be too tight

Slip Stitch Pattern

Rnd 1: (C2) *k3, sl 1, rep from *
Rnd 2: (C2) *p3, sl 1 wyib, rep from *
Rnd 3: (C1) k1, *sl 1, k3, rep from *; end k2
Rnd 4: (C1) k1, *sl 1, k3, rep from *; end k2

Materials
1 skein (MC)
1 skein (CC)
Set of dpns at least two sizes larger than those used to get gauge in st st

Directions

CO with MC and work k2, p2 rib for 14 rounds. Switch to larger ndls. Knit 1 rnd. Rep these 4 rounds for 6" or desired length to top of ankle bone. Switch back to smaller ndls.

Work heel in CC, foot in MC and toe in CC.

Rib Stitch

Irene's Cable

Slip Stitch

Girly Socks
design by Mary McSweeny

Finished Sizes
XS, S, M

Gauge 5 sts = 1"

Materials
1 skein Superwash (MC)
1 skein Superwash (CC)

Pattern 187

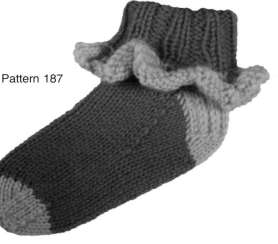

Directions

CO 96 (120, 144) sts with CC. Join, being careful not to twist the circle. Purl 4 (4, 5) rnds. On Rnd 5 (5, 6), *p3tog around. Purl one rnd. Switch to MC and purl one rnd. Work k2, p2 ribbing for 35 (40, 45) rnds or to desired length. Knit 8 (10, 12) sts.

Heel

Switch to contrast color, if desired. Purl (16, 20, 24) sts (WS).
Row 1: *sl 1 as if to purl; k1. Rep from * across heel stitches only. Turn work.
Row 2: sl 1 as if to purl, purl to end.
Rep these rows 7 (9, 11) times for a total of 14 (18, 22) rows. Work row 1 again.

Turn Heel & Gusset

Purl 10 (12, 14) sts, p2tog, p1; turn
Sl 1 as if to purl, k5, k2tog, k1; turn

Sl 1 as if to purl, p6, p2tog, p1; turn
Sl 1 as if to purl, k7, k2tog, k1; turn
Sl 1 as if to purl, p8, p2tog, p1; turn

Continue alternating knit and purl rows, knitting or purling the st before the gap with the st after the gap, until all of the sts have been used. In the second-to-last row, you will k2tog, but not have a stitch to knit or slip. Turn the work, knit to the last 2 sts, and knit them together.

Along the side of the heel flap rectangle you just made, pick up and knit the edge

sts from back to front (8, 10, 12 sts) and the slip sts made at the beginning of each heel flap row. You may also want to pick up a st before and after these slip sts to avoid holes at the ankles. Knit these sts onto the heel flap needle. Knit the stitches across the top of the foot.

Pick up the same number of sts on the other side of the heel flap and knit them. Knit 5 (6, 7) sts from heel onto the same needle. Knit one rnd.

Gusset decreases

Knit to the last three sts on ndl 1, k2tog, k1. Knit across ndl 2 On ndl 3, k1, ssk, knit the remaining sts. Knit one rnd. Repeat decrease rnd and plain rnd until there are 32 (40, 48) sts.
Knit until sock comes to the little toe. Begin decreasing for the toe as follows:

Rnd 1

Ndl 1: knit to last three sts; k2tog, k1
Ndl 2: k1, ssk, knit to last three sts; k2tog, k1
Ndl 3: k1, ssk, knit rem sts

Rnd 2: knit

Repeat these rnds until 12 sts remain. Knit three sts from ndl 1 onto ndl 3. Cut tail and graft toe with kitchener stitch.

Variation: Picot Top Socks

Directions

*CO 6 sts with CC; then bind off 2 sts. Move st from right ndl to left ndl; rep from * until 32 (40, 48) sts have been cast on. Join into rnd, being careful not to twist the circle. Purl one row. Switch to MC; purl one row. Work k2, p2 ribbing for 35 (40, 45) rnds or to desired length. Knit 8 (10, 12) sts.

Work the heel and the foot as described in the main pattern.

Variation: Daisy Top Socks

Directions

*CO 9 (10, 11) sts with CC; then bind off 7 (8, 9) sts. Move st on right ndl back to left ndl; rep from * until 32 (40, 48) sts have been cast on. Join into round, being careful not to twist the circle. Purl one row. Switch to MC; purl one row. Work k2, p2 rib for 35 (40, 45) rnds or to desired length. Knit 8 (10, 12) sts.

Work the heel and the foot as described in the main pattern.

Variation: Bobble Top Socks
Directions

*CO 2 sts with CC. [K1, p1] 3 times into st; turn work, ignoring the other st. Knit 6 sts; turn work; purl 6 sts; turn work and knit 6 sts again. Turn work; sl 3, one at a time, to the right ndl, p3tog, and pull the 3 slipped st, one at a time, over the one made from p3tog. Move the st on the right ndl back to the left ndl. Rep from * until 32 (40, 48) sts have been cast on.

Join into round, being careful not to twist the circle. Purl one row. Switch to MC and purl one row. Work k2, p2 rib for 35 (40, 45) rnds or to desired length. Knit 8 (10, 12) sts. Work the heel and the foot as described in the main pattern.

Variation: Lacy Petal Top
Directions

CO 4 sts with CC. Work petals as follows:

Row 1: purl
Row 2: k1, yo, k2, yo, k1
Row 3: purl
Row 4: k1, yo, k4, yo, k1
Row 5: purl.

Cut yarn. Hold ndl with petal in right hand, CO for a second petal. Make 4 (5, 6) petals total; do not cut yarn after last petal. Join into rnd with knit side in and purl side out. Purl 1 rnd. Switch to MC and purl one row.

Work k2, p2 ribbing for 35 (40, 45) rnds or to desired length. Knit 8 (10, 12) sts.

Work the heel and the foot as described in the main pattern.

Pattern 188

Pattern 189

Pattern 190

Pattern 191

Mitza Coat

design by Mary Lou Egan

Finished sizes
Finished chest sizes 44, 48, 50, 52"
Finished length about 27". The jacket will lengthen a bit with wearing

Gauge
4 sts x 8 rows = 1" worked double-stranded in Raised Brick Stitch. Knit a generous swatch (at least 5" x 5") and block it, stretching it slightly. Let dry, then measure gauge.

Materials
15 (15, 16, 16) skeins #9454 (Plum Heather)
US 9 (5.5 mm) 32" circ ndl
US 10 ½ (6.5 mm) 32" circ ndl (or size needed to obtain gauge)
3 toggle buttons
4 flat ¾" or 1" buttons

Raised Brick Stitch
Note: Slip all sts purlwise
Row 1: (RS) k3, *sl 1 wyib, k3, rep to end
Row 2: k3, * sl1 wyif, k3
Row 3: k1, sl 1 wyib, *k3, sl 1, rep from *; end k1
Row 4: k1, sl 1 wyif, *k3, sl 1, rep. from *; end k1

Directions
CO 88 (96, 100, 104) sts with smaller ndl and 2 strands of yarn. Work in Brick Stitch for 3". Change to larger ndl and continue until piece measures 15" **Note: you can alter coat length by knitting a few inches more or less at this point.**
Begin increasing for arms as follows: CO 4 sts on each side of every RS row 11 (11, 10, 10) times, then 6 sts every RS row 4 times.

Work even for 5". Work neck as follows: work 68 (68, 64, 64) sleeves sts, 30 (34, 35, 37) body sts, and then bind off 28 (28, 30, 30) sts for neckline. Work to end of row. Each side is now worked separately.

Right front
Work in Raised Brick Stitch for 1". Begin increasing at neck edge by knitting in the front and back of the first st, every other row, until 29 (29, 28, 30) sts are added. At the same time, when sleeve cuff measures 10", begin binding off the sleeve as follows: bind off 6 sts 4 times, then 4 sts 11 times. Work even until the same length as the back. Bind off in knit on a WS row.

Left front
Work as for right front, reversing shaping.

Pattern 192

Finishing
Fold in half as shown in schematic. With right sides together, sew seams along sleeves and sides of body, matching sts and ridges, and leaving 3 to 3½" of the side seams open at the hem. Turn right side out. With RS facing, work applied I-cord along front and neck, picking up 1 st for each ridge, and making 3 I-cord buttonhole loops as shown in photo.

To make the buttonhole loops, work about 1½" of I-cord, twist it, and secure it by working the next I-cord st into the base of the loop. When finished, twist the loop and sew it down. On the left side, work 1" of unattached I-cord 1" below the end of neck shaping (see schematic), or alternatively, crochet a chain loop. This buttonhole secures the underside of the jacket fronts.

Try the sweater on for button placement. Sew buttons into place, with flat button underneath for reinforcement. Sew the flat button on the WS to match buttonhole for the left front. Be sure the flat button doesn't show through to RS.

Variation: Mitza Coat with Shawl Collar
Materials
6 (6, 7, 7) skeins #8401(Silver Grey; C1)
5 skeins #8555 (Black; C2)
5 skeins #8400 (Charcoal Grey; C3)
3 buttons
4 flat ¾" or 1" buttons

Directions
CO with 2 strands of C1 and work coat in Raised Brick Stitch as described in the main pattern. Work 2 rows in C1, 2 rows in C2, and 2 rows in C3. Continue this color sequence throughout.

Border and collar
With C1, pick up 1 st for each garter stitch ridge along the front, pm 3" below point where increasing ended on right front, pick up 1 st for each bound-off st at back neck, pick up 1 st for each garter stitch ridge along the front, pm at point where increasing ended on the left front.

Work short rows as follows: turn and knit back. After working across the back neck sts, *wrap and turn, k5, m1, k2; rep from * 9 times, k5. On the next row, wrap and turn, sl 1, knit across to wrapped st, knit it, wrap and turn. Rep for a total of 17 times.

Wrap and turn, knit across to wrapped st, knit it, k4, wrap and turn; repeat 4 times. Wrap and turn, knit across entire front of sweater, turn, work I-cord bind-off.

At each marker, work 3 rows of unattached I-cord for buttonholes. Continue for entire edge of sweater. Try the sweater on for button placement. Sew buttons into place, with flat button underneath for reinforcement. Sew the flat button on the WS to match buttonhole for the left front.

Cartridge Belt Rib Coat
Materials
13 (13, 14, 14) skeins #2401 (Burgandy)

Cartridge Belt Rib (multiple of 4 sts + 3)
Row 1: k3, *sl 1 wyif, k3, rep from *
Row 2: k1, *sl 1 wyif, k3, rep from * to last 2 sts, sl 1, k1

Directions
Work coat as described in the main pattern, but working Cartridge Belt Rib instead of Raised Brick Stitch.

Finishing
Using smaller ndl, pick up 3 sts for every 4 rows along right front. At the point where increasing stopped, pm, pick up 1 st in point, pm. Continue picking up 3 sts for every 4 rows, then 1 st for each bound-off st on neck back, and 3 sts for every 4 rows along left front.
Row 1 (WS): purl
Row 2: knit, working m1 on either side of the marked st
Row 3: purl
Row 4: knit, work m1 on either side of marked st
Row 5: knit
Row 6: knit, working k2tog on either side of the marked st
Row 7: purl
Row 8: knit, working k2tog on either side of the marked st
Row 9: purl
Bind off. Fold at ridge, and sew in place.

Mark the placement for buttons on left front. Make I-cord buttonhole loops. Sew loops and buttons, sewing the flat buttons underneath for reinforcement. Crochet a chain loop on left front border at the same point as the toggle on the right front. Sew a flat button on the WS of the left front to match up with the buttonhole on right front. This buttonhole secures the underside of the jacket fronts.

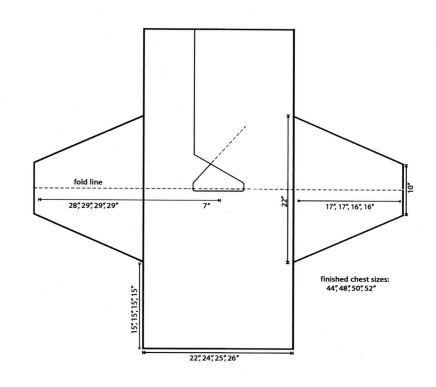

finished chest sizes:
44", 48", 50", 52"

fold line
28", 29", 29", 29"
7"
17", 17", 16", 16"
10"
22"
15", 15", 15", 15"
22", 24", 25", 26"

Coat with Stand-Up Collar
Materials
16 (16, 17, 17) skeins #2438 (Mimosa)

Directions
Work coat double-stranded in Raised Brick Stitch as described in the main pattern until the fronts are worked separately. After binding off the neck back sts, work 4 rows, then begin increasing at neck edge by knitting into the front and back of the st, every other row 17 times. Then CO 2 sts at neck edge every other row 7 times. Work even until the same length as the back.

Finishing
On each side, place a safety pin along the neck edge, 7" from dividing row. Beginning at this point, work applied I-cord along the neck edge (20 sts on right side, 28 back sts, and 19 sts on left side). With smaller ndl, attach yarn, and pick up and knit one st for each row of I-cord through the back st of the cord.

Pattern 193

Work 1¾" in Raised Brick Stitch, decreasing 1 st at neck edge each side every other row 2 times. Leave sts on ndl. Mark points on the front where increasing ended, and at the base of the collar on the right front. Beginning at the hem on the right front, work applied I-cord along the front and neck of the sweater. At the marked points, work 3 rows of unattached I-cord for buttonholes. Sew on toggle buttons, with flat buttons underneath for reinforcement.

Worsted-Weight Mitza Coat
Gauge
6 sts = 1" worked single-stranded in Raised Brick Stitch

Materials
10 (11, 12, 12) skeins #9450 (Smoke Heather)
US 7 (mm) 32" circ ndl
US 8 (mm) 32" circ ndl (or size needed to obtain gauge)

Directions
With smaller needles, CO 111 (123, 127, 131) sts. Work in Raised Brick Stitch for 3". Change to larger ndl and work for 15" total.

Note: you can alter coat length by knitting a few inches more or less at this point.

Begin increasing for arms as follows: CO 6 sts on each side of RS row 11 (11, 10, 10) times, then 9 sts every RS row 4 times.

Work even for 5" inches. Work neck as follows: work 102 (102, 96, 96) sleeves sts, 44 (52, 54, 58) body sts, bind off 37 (37, 37, 37) sts for neckline, work to end of row. Each side is now worked separately.

Right front
Work in Raised Brick Stitch for 1". Begin increasing at neck edge by knitting into the front and back of the first st, every other row, until 47 (47, 49, 49) sts have been added. At the same time, when sleeve cuff measures 10", begin binding off the sleeve as follows: bind off 9 sts 4 times, then 6 stitches 11 times. Work even until the same length as the back. Bind off in knit on WS row.

Work left front and finish as described in the main pattern.

Pattern 194

Pattern 195

Pattern 196

80

Gloves

design by Elizabeth Wellenstein

Finished Sizes
Adult S (L) is 8 (9.3)" in circumference

Gauge
6 sts x 7rnds = 1" worked in st st on larger ndl in the rnd

Materials
1 skein #9456 (Sapphire Heather)
Set of US 3 (3.25 mm) dpns
Set of US 5 (3.75 mm) dpns, or size to obtain gauge.

Directions
Cuff
With smaller dpns, CO 40 (48) sts. You will have 10 (12) sts on each ndl. Join ends, being careful not to twist circle. Pm between first and second st to secure. Work k2, p2 rib for 2½ (3)" from cast-on edge. Change to larger ndls and knit one rnd. Increase as follows: inc 4 sts evenly in next rnd to 44 (52) sts. Knit one rnd. Inc 4 sts evenly in next rnd to 48 (56) sts. Knit 1¾ (2¼)" from top of rib or until you reach the base of the thumb.

Note: The back of the glove is worked on ndls 1 and 2, and the palm is worked on ndls 3 and 4.

Right thumb placement
Knit 27 (31) sts. Knit the next 9 (10) sts with a piece of waste yarn. Slip waste yarn sts back to LHN and knit again with working yarn. Knit until piece measures 1¾ (2)" from waste yarn.

Right Hand Fingers
Beginning at pinky edge, k5 (6). Place next 38 (44) sts on a piece of waste yarn. These sts will be worked separately, one finger at a time. With another needle, CO 2 (3) sts to join pinky front to back. Work remaining 5 (6) sts. Rearrange sts evenly on dpns. Knit around until finger measures 2 (2½)" or ¼" shorter than desired length. To shape, k2tog around. Slip yarn through rem sts and pull closed. Pull tail to inside, secure, and weave in end. Before knitting ring finger, pick up 2 (3) sts in cast-on edge of pinky. Place sts currently on hold back on ndls. Knit around for ½" from cast-on edge of pinky.

Ring Finger
Beginning at ring finger edge, k8 (10) sts. Place next 26 (30) sts on a piece of waste yarn. With another ndl, CO 2 (3) to join finger front to back. Knit rem 6 (7) sts on round. Rearrange sts evenly on dpns. Knit around until finger measures 2½ (3)", or ¼" shorter than desired length. To shape, k2tog around once (twice). Slip yarn through rem sts and pull closed. Pull tail to inside and secure.

Middle Finger
Beginning at cast-on edge of ring finger, pick up 2 (3) sts in cast-on edge of ring finger. Place first 6 (7) sts from waste yarn onto ndl. With another ndl, CO 2 (3) sts to join finger front to back. Pick up last 6 (7) sts from waste yarn to complete back of finger. Rearrange sts evenly on dpns. Knit around until finger measures 2¾ (3¼)", or ¼" shorter than desired length. To shape, k2tog around once (twice). Slip yarn through rem sts and pull closed. Pull tail to inside, secure and weave in end.

Index Finger
Beginning at cast-on edge of middle finger, pick up 2 (3) sts in cast on edge of middle finger. Place half of the sts from waste yarn onto ndl. With another ndl, pick up rem sts from waste yarn to complete back of finger. Rearrange sts evenly on dpns. Knit around until finger measures 2½ (3)", or ¼" shorter than desired length. To shape, k2tog around once (twice). Slip yarn through rem sts and pull closed. Pull tail to inside, secure and weave in end.

Left thumb placement
Knit 36 (43) sts. Knit next 9 (10) sts with a piece of waste yarn (for thumb opening). Slip waste yarn sts back to LHN and knit again with working yarn. Finish rnd.

Left Hand Fingers
Before knitting index finger, knit across 19 (22) sts. Place next 10 (12) sts (pinky sts) on a piece of waste yarn. With another needle, CO 2 (3) sts to join ring finger front to back and knit to end of rnd.

Pattern 197

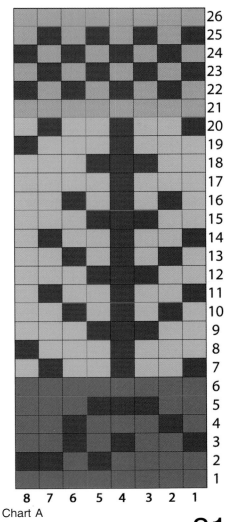

Chart A

8 7 6 5 4 3 2 1

26 25 24 23 22 21 20 19 18 17 16 15 14 13 12 11 10 9 8 7 6 5 4 3 2 1

Knit around for ½" from the waste yarn of pinky.

Index Finger
Beginning at index edge, k7 (8). Place next 24 (28) sts on a second piece of waste yarn. With another ndl, CO 2 (3) sts to join index front to back. Knit rem 7 (8) sts. Finish same as right index finger.

Middle Finger
Beginning at cast-on edge of index finger, pick up 2 (3) sts in cast on edge of index finger. Place first 6 (7) sts from waste yarn onto ndl. With another ndl, CO 2 (3) sts to join middle finger front to back. Pick up the last 6 (7) sts from the waste yarn to complete back of finger. Finish same as right middle finger.

Ring Finger
Beginning at cast-on edge of middle finger, pick 2 (3) sts in cast-on edge of middle finger. Place half of the sts from waste yarn onto ndl. With another ndl, pick up rem sts from waste yarn to complete back of finger. Do not include separate pinky sts. Finish same as right ring finger.

Pinky
Beginning at cast on edge of ring finger, pick up 2 (3) sts in cast on edge of ring finger. Place half of the sts from pinky waste yarn onto ndl. With another ndl, pick up rem sts from waste yarn to complete back of finger. Finish same as right pinky.

Thumb Finishing
Pick out waste yarn at thumb and place live sts on 2 ndls. Sts should be picked up from left to right, if right-handed. There will be 8 (9) sts on top, 9 (10) sts on bottom. Pm to identify beg of rnd. Pick up and knit into the back of the corner st to close up gap. Knit across 9 (10) sts on bottom. Pick up and knit into the back of corner st. Knit across 8 (9) sts (19, 21 sts on ndls). Join and knit around until thumb is 2 (2½)" or ¼" shorter than desired length. To shape, k2tog around twice. Slip yarn through rem sts and pull closed. Pull tail to inside and secure.

Variation: Fingerless Gloves
Materials
1 skein #7803 (Magenta)

Directions
Work Basic Glove as described in the main pattern. Work fingers and thumbs to desired length, either just before or just after the first knuckle. Work 2 rnds of k1,

p1 ribbing at the top. Some fingers may have an odd number of sts and require a k2tog to work the ribbing. Bind off in ribbing.

Variation: 3-Color Gloves
Materials
1 skein each #8010 (Natural; C1), #8888 (Lavender; C2), #8887 (Dark Lavender; C3)

Gauge
6 sts x 7 rows =1" worked in color pattern in the round

Directions
Work Basic Glove as described in the main pattern, using C3 (background color). Work until increase rnds are complete. **Note:** if you are knitting the larger size, work 2 additional rnds in background color to center colorwork.

Work Chart A. Work a solid rnd of background color for thumb placement then work another repeat of Chart A. Finish as for Basic Glove in background color.

Variation: 4-Color Gloves
Materials
1 skein each #8887 (Dark Lavender; C1), #7803 (Magenta; C2), #9444 (Tangerine Heather; C3), and #7814 (Chartreuse; C4)

Gauge
6.5 sts x 6.5 rows = 1" in color pattern worked in the round

Directions
Work Basic Glove as described in the main pattern, using C1 (background color). Work until increase rnds are complete. **Note:** if you are knitting the larger size, work 2 additional rnds in background color to center colorwork.

Work Chart B. Finish in background color as described in the main pattern.

Variation: Cabled Gloves
Finished size
Slightly less than 8" circumference

Materials
1 skein #7803 (Magenta)
Set of US 4 (3.5 mm) and US 5 (3.75 mm) dpns

Directions
With US 4 ndls, CO 41 sts. Join work, being careful not to twist the circle. Pm between the first and second st to secure.

Rnd 1: k2, p2, pm (to mark cable), k15, pm, p2, *k2, p2; rep from *
Rnd 2: k2, p2, k15, p2, *k2, p2; rep from *
Rnd 3: k2, p2, k3, c6f, c6f, p2, *k2, p2; rep from *
Rnd 4: k2, p2, k15, p2, *k2, p2; rep from *
Rnd 5 and 6: rep rnds 1 and 2
Rnd 7: k2, p2, c6b, c6b, k3, p2, *k2, p2; rep from *
Rnd 8: k2, p2, k15, p2, *k2, p2; rep from *

Rep rnds 1-8 for an approx 2" cuff. Change to larger ndls and knit one rnd (continue to cable in pattern). Increase 4 sts evenly in next rnd, outside of the 15 cable sts, while continuing to work the cable until beginning of fingers (45 sts). Work 1 rnd. Inc 3 sts evenly in next rnd (48 sts). Knit 1¾" from top of ribbing or until you reach the base of the thumb. Work as described for the smaller size of the main pattern, beginning at the right thumb placement.

Cable Pattern

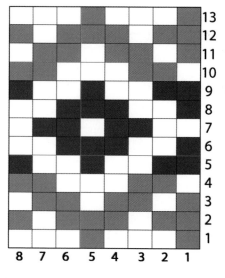

Chart B

Popovers
design by Elizabeth Wellenstein

Finished sizes
Adult S (L) finished circumference is 8 (9.3)"

Gauge
6 sts x 7 rnds = 1" worked on larger ndl in st st in the rnd

Materials
1 skein #9429 (Mossy Rock)
Set of US 5 (3.75 mm) dpns (or size to obtain gauge)
Set of US 3 (3.25 mm) dpns

Directions
Cuff
CO 40 (48) sts with smaller dpns. Join ends, being careful not to twist sts and pm between first and second st to secure. Work k2, p2 rib for 2½ (3)" from cast on edge. Change to larger dpns. Knit one rnd, then inc 4 sts evenly in next rnd to 44 (52) sts. Knit one rnd, inc 4 more sts evenly in next rnd to 48 (56) sts. Knit 1¾ (2¼)" from top of rib or until you reach the base of the thumb.

Right Thumb Placement
Note: The back of the gauntlet is worked on ndls 1 and 2 and the palm is worked on ndls 3 and 4.
Knit 27 (31) sts. Knit the next 9 (10) sts with a piece of waste yarn. Slip waste yarn sts back to LHN and knit again with working yarn. Finish rnd.

Left Thumb Placement
Knit 36 (43) sts. Knit the next 9 (10) sts with a piece of waste yarn. Slip waste yarn sts back to LHN and knit again with working yarn. Finish rnd.

Create a purl ridge for the attachment of the popover. Knit around until piece measures 1 (1¼)" from waste yarn. Purl sts on the back of the gauntlet and knit the sts on the palm. Knit around for 2" or to desired length. Work in k2, p2 rib for 1". Cast off loosely in rib.

Thumb Finishing
Pick out waste yarn at thumb and place live sts on 2 ndls: 8 (9) sts on top, 9 (10) sts on bottom. Sts should be picked up from left to right, if right handed. Pm for beg of rnd. Pick up and knit into the back of corner st to close up gap. Knit 9 (10) sts across bottom. Pick up and knit into

Pattern 202

the back of corner st. Knit 8 (9) sts (19, 21 total sts). Distribute sts evenly on 3 dpns and work in k1, p1 rib for 1" or to desired length. Cast off loosely in rib.

Popover
With 1st dpn and back of gauntlet facing, pick up 1 st in each purl bump across the first 12 (14) sts of the back. Pick up rem purl bumps with second dpn. With third dpn, cast on 24 (28) sts and place half of them on a fourth dpn.
Rnd 1: k1, inc 1, knit to last 2 sts on back, inc 1, k1, k across 24 (28) palm sts
Rnd 2: knit across back 26 (30) sts, work k2, p2 ribbing across 24 (28) palm sts
Continue as established, knitting across the back, rib across the palm, until rib measures 1" (50, 58 sts). Knit around until popover measures 2¾ (3½)" from rib, or about 1½ (2)" shorter than desired length. Decrease for top as follows:

Rnd 1: *k23 (27), k2tog; rep from * 48 (56) sts
Rnd 2: *k10 (12), k2tog; rep from * 44 (52) sts
Rnd 3: *k9 (11), k2tog; rep from * 40 (48) sts
Continue as established, working one less st between the decreases, until 8 sts

or fewer remain. Cut yarn, leaving an approx 12" tail. Slip yarn through rem sts and pull closed. Pull tail to inside, secure and weave in end.

Optional: You may want to secure the top half of the popover when it is folded back, so that it doesn't flop around. Do this by attaching a small loop of yarn at the tip. Fold the top back and sew a small button where the loop meets the back of the wrist.

Variation: Popover Fingerless Gloves
Materials
1 skein #7808 (Purple Hyacinth)

Directions
Work popovers as described in the main pattern until the purl ridge for the popover is complete. Knit around for ¾ " from purl ridge.

Right-hand fingers
Note: Work fingers to desired length, either just before or just after the first knuckle. Work 2 rnds of k1, p1 rib at the top. Some fingers may have an odd

number of sts and require a k2tog to support the ribbing. Bind off in ribbing.

Beginning at pinky edge, k5 (6) sts. Place the next 38 (44) sts on a piece of waste yarn. These sts will be worked separately, one finger at a time. With another ndl, CO 2 (3) sts to join pinky front to back. Work rem 5 (6) sts. Rearrange sts evenly on dpns. Work pinky finger to desired length and finish as described above. Before knitting ring finger, pick up 2(3) sts in cast-on edge of pinky. Place sts currently on hold back on ndls. Knit around for ½" from cast-on edge of pinky.

Ring finger
Beginning at ring finger edge, k8 (10) sts. Place next 26 (30) sts on a piece of waste yarn. With another ndl, CO 2 (3) to join finger front to back. Knit rem 6 (7) sts on rnd. Rearrange sts evenly on dpns. Work finger to desired length and finish as described above.

Middle finger
Pick up 2 (3) sts in cast-on edge of ring finger. Place first 6 (7) sts from waste yarn onto ndl. With another ndl, CO 2 (3) sts to join finger front to back. Pick up last 6 (7) sts from waste yarn to complete the back of the finger. Rearrange sts evenly on dpns. Work finger to desired length and finish as described above.

Index finger
Pick up 2 (3) sts in cast-on edge of middle finger. Place half of the sts from waste yarn onto ndl. With another ndl, pick up rem sts from waste yarn to complete the back of the finger. Rearrange sts evenly on dpns. Work finger to desired length and finish as described above.

Left-hand fingers
Before knitting index finger, knit across 19 (22). Place next 10 (12) sts (pinky sts) on a piece of waste yarn. With another needle, CO 2 (3) sts to join ring finger front to back. Knit to end of rnd. Knit around for ½" from the waste yarn of pinky.

Index Finger
Beginning at index edge, k7 (8) sts. Place next 24 (28) sts on a second piece of waste yarn. With another ndl, CO 2 (3) sts to join index front to back. Knit rem 7 (8) sts. Work finger to desired length and finish as described above.

Middle Finger
Pick up 2 (3) sts in cast-on edge of index finger. Place first 6 (7) sts from waste yarn onto ndl. With another ndl, CO 2(3) sts to join middle finger front to back. Pick up the last 6 (7) sts from the waste yarn to complete the back of the finger. Work finger to desired length and finish as described above.

Ring Finger
Pick up 2 (3) sts in cast-on edge of middle finger. Place half of the sts from waste yarn onto ndl. With another ndl, pick up rem sts from waste yarn to complete the back of the finger. Don't include separate pinky sts. Work finger to desired length and finish as described above.

Pinky
Pick up 2 (3) sts in cast-on edge of ring finger. Place half of the sts from pinky waste yarn onto ndl. With another ndl, pick up rem sts from waste yarn to complete the back of the finger. Work finger to desired length and finish as described above.

Thumb finishing
Pick out waste yarn at thumb and place live sts on 2 ndls: 8 (9) sts on top, 9 (10) sts on bottom. Sts should be picked up from left to right, if right handed. Pm for beg of rnd. Pick up and knit into the back of corner st to close up gap. Knit across 9 (10) sts on bottom. Pick up and knit into the back of corner st. Knit across 8 (9) sts (19, 21 total sts). Distribute sts evenly on 3 dpns and work in k1, p1 rib for 1" or to desired length. Cast off loosely in rib.

Work popover as described in the main pattern.

Variation: Checked Popovers
Materials
1 skein #2401 (Burgandy; C1)
1 skein #8234 (Pistachio; C2)

Directions
CO with C1 and work as described in the main pattern until increase rnds are complete. Attach C2 and work Rows 1-4 of Chart A 5 (6) times.

With C2, create the purl ridge for the attachment of the popover and finish as either as gauntlets or as fingerless gloves, working the popover with C2 and the thumb with C1.

Variation: Two-Color Popovers
Materials
1 skein #8555 (Black; C1)
1 skein #8234 (Pistachio; C2)

Directions
CO with C1 and work as described in the main pattern until increase rnds are complete. Attach C2 and knit 1 rnd. Work Rows 1-8 of Chart B 2 (3) times. If you are knitting the smaller size, knit Rows 1-3 from Chart B again. For both sizes, knit 1 rnd with C2.

With C1, create the purl ridge for the attachment of the popover. Continue as described in the main pattern, either as gauntlets or as fingerless gloves, using C1 for the popover and the thumb.

Variation: Pines in Purls Popover
Materials
1 ½ skeins #8400 (Charcoal Grey)

Directions
Work as described in the main pattern until the increase rnds are complete. Work Rows 1-21 of Chart C, working the dots in the chart as purls sts. If you are knitting the larger size, knit 3 plain rnds before starting purl ridge.

Continue as described in the main pattern, either as gauntlets or as fingerless gloves.

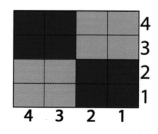

Chart A

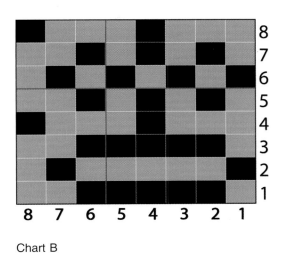

Chart B

knit

purl

Chart C

Variety Socks

design by Mary McSweeny

Finished size S (M, L)

Gauge 5 sts = 1"

Materials
2 skeins Superwash
Set of US 3 (3.25 mm) dpns

Lace Rib
Rnd 1: *p2, yo, (sl 1, k1, psso), p2, k2; rep from *
Rnd 2: *p2, k2, rep from *
Rnd 3: *p2, k2tog, yo, p2, k2; rep from *
Rnd 4: *p2, k2, rep from *

Directions
CO 40 (48, 56) sts; join into round, being careful not to twist the sts. Work Lace Rib for 6" or to desired length.

Heel
Note: Instructions for the heel and foot are given for 40 (42, 48, 54, 56) sts to cover each variation

Knit 10 (10, 12, 14, 14) sts; turn work. Purl 20 (20, 24, 28, 28) sts.

Pattern 207

85

Heel Row 1 (RS): *Sl 1 as if to purl; k1, rep from * across heel stitches only
Heel Row 2: Sl 1 as if to purl; purl to end of heel sts
Repeat Heel Rows 1 and 2 for 9 (9, 11, 13, 13) times, for a total of 18 (18, 22, 26, 26) rows, then rep Heel Row 1 again.

Turn Heel & Gusset

Purl 12 (12, 14, 16, 16) sts, p2tog; p1, turn
Sl 1 as if to purl, k5, k2tog, k1, turn
Sl 1 as if to purl, p6, p2tog, p1, turn
Sl 1 as if to purl, k7, k2tog, k1, turn
Sl 1 as if to purl, p8, p2tog, p1, turn
Cont alternating knit and purl rows, knitting or purling the st before the gap with the st after the gap, until all of the sts have been used. In the second-to-last row, you will k2tog, but not have a st to knit or slip. Turn the work, knit to the last 2 sts, and knit them together.

Along the side of the heel flap rectangle you just made, pick up the edge sts from back to front. There should be 10 (10, 11, 12, 12) sts and the slip sts made at the beginning of each heel flap row. In addition, you may want to pick up a st before and after these slip sts to avoid holes at the ankles. Knit these sts onto the heel flap needle.

Knit the sts across the top of the foot. Continue in pattern across instep, if desired. Pick up and knit the same number of sts on this side of the heel flap as the other side. Knit 6 (6, 7, 8, 8) sts from heel onto the same needle. Knit one rnd.

Gusset decreases

Knit to last three sts on ndl #1, k2tog, k1.
Knit across ndl #2. On ndl #3, k1, ssk, knit the remaining sts. Knit one rnd. Rep the decrease row and knit row until there are 40 (42, 48, 54, 56) sts.

Foot

Knit until sock comes to the little toe. Decrease for the toe as follows:
Rnd 1
Ndl 1: knit to last three sts, k2tog, k1
Ndl 2: k1, ssk, knit to last three sts, k2tog, k1
Ndl 3: k1, ssk, knit rem sts
Rnd 2 : Knit
Work rnds 1 and 2 until 12 sts remain. Knit three sts from ndl 1 onto ndl 3. Graft toe with kitchener stitch.

Variation: Mini-Cabled Socks
Materials
2 skeins

Mini-Cable Stitch
Rnds 1 and 2: *k3, p1, rep from *
Rnd 3: *knit 3rd st on left ndl, then second st, then first st, sl all three sts off left ndl, p1, rep from *
Rnds 4-7: *k3, p1, rep from *

Directions
CO 40 (48, 56) sts. Join into round, being careful not to twist sts. Work rows 1-7 of Mini-Cable Stitch once, then work rows 3-7 of the pattern for 6" or to desired length. Work heel and foot as described in the main pattern.

Variation: Snake Rib and Openwork
Materials
2 skeins

Snake Rib
Rnds 1 and 2: *k2, p2, rep from *
Rnd 3: *k2tog, yo, p2, rep from *
Rnds 4-6: *k2, p2, rep from *
Rnd 7: *yo, k2tog, p2, rep from *
Rnds 8-10: *k2, p2, rep from *

CO 40 (48, 56) sts. Join into round, being careful not to twist sts. Work rnds 1-10 of Snake Rib once, then work rnds 3-10 for 6" or to desired length. Work heel and foot as described in the main pattern.

Variation: Hugs and Kisses
Materials
2 skeins

Hugs and Kisses Stitch
Rows 1 and 2:*k4, p2, rep from *
Row 3: * c2b, c2f, p2, rep from *
Row 4: *k4, p2, rep from *
Row 5: * c2b, c2f, p2, rep from *
Row 6: *k4, p2, rep from *
Row 7: * c2f, c2b, p2, rep from *
Row 8: *k4, p2, rep from *
Row 9: * c2f, c2b, p2, rep from *
Row 10: *k4, p2, rep from *

Directions
CO 42 (48, 54) sts. Join, being careful not to twist the circle. Work Rnds 1-10 of Hugs and Kisses Stitch once, then work Rnds 3-10 for 6" or to desired length. Work heel and foot as described in the main pattern.

Variation: Openwork Ribbed Socks
Materials
2 skein

Openwork Rib Stitch
Row 1: *p1, k2tog, yo twice, (sl 1, k1, psso), rep from *
Row 2: *p1, k2, p1, k1, p1, rep from *
Rows 3 and 4: *p1, k4, p1, rep from *

Directions
CO 42 (48, 54) sts. Join, being careful not to twist the circle. Work Openwork Rib Stitch for 6" or to desired length. Work heel and foot as described in the main pattern.

Pattern 208

Pattern 209

Pattern 210

Pattern 211

Textured Scarves

design by Patti Pierce Stone

Finished size
About 8" x 72"

Gauge is not important for this pattern

Materials
2 skeins #2438 (Spring Meadow)
US 7 (4.5 mm) ndl

Slip Stitch Pattern
Note: slip all sts purlwise wyif
Row 1 (RS): k2, [p1, k1] twice. [sl 1, k3] 8 times; end sl 1, [k1, p1] twice, sl 2 wyif
Row 2: k2, [p1, k1] twice. [sl 1, p3] 8 times; end sl 1, [k1, p1] twice, sl 2 wyif
Row 3: k3, p1, k1, p1. k2, [sl 1, k3] 7 times; end sl 1, k2, [p1, k1] twice, sl 2 wyif
Row 4: k3, p1, k1, p1. k2, [sl 1, k3] 7 times. end sl 1, k2, [p1, k1] twice, sl 2 wyif

Double Seed Stitch Border
Rows 1 and 2: k3. *p1, k1 to last 2 sts, sl 2 wyif
Rows 3 and 4: k2. *p1, k1 to last 3 sts on row; end p1, sl 2 wyif

Directions
CO 45 sts with a long-tail cast-on method. Work rows 1-4 of Double Seed Stitch Border Pattern, then work rows 1-2 again. Then work rows 1-4 of Slip Stitch Pattern until the scarf measures 71" from cast-on edge or 1" shorter than desired length. Finish by working rows 1-4, then rows 1-2 of Slip Stitch Pattern. Cast off evenly.

Variation: Raised Brick Stitch Scarf
Materials
2 skeins #9419 (Vermeer Blue)

Raised Brick Stitch
Note: Slip all sts purlwise
Row 1: (RS) k3, *sl 1 wyib, k3, rep to end
Row 2: k3, *sl1 wyif, k3
Row 3: k1, sl 1 wyib, *k3, sl 1, rep from *; end k1
Row 4: k1, sl 1 wyif, *k3, sl 1, rep. from *; end k1

Directions
CO 45 sts. Work 6 rows of a garter stitch border as follows: knit to last 3 sts, sl 3 wyif. Work Raised Brick Stitch until the scarf measures 71" from cast-on edge or 1" shorter than desired length. Finish with 6 rows of garter border.

Pattern 213

Pattern 212

Pattern 214

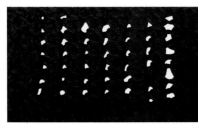

Pattern 215

Variation: Herringbone Scarf
Materials
2 skeins #2414 (Russet)
US 7 (4.5 mm) ndl
US 9 (5.5 mm) ndl (or size needed to maintain gauge of the border rows)

Herringbone Stitch
Row 1 (WS): k2, p1, k1, p1, p2tog slipping only the first loop off the non-working ndl. *Purl tog the st on the ndl and the next st. Rep from * to last 5 sts (the first st will be the leftover from the last p2tog); end p1 tbl, k1, p1, sl 2 wyif
Row 2: k2, p1, k1, p1, k2tog tbl slipping only the first loop off the non-working ndl. * Knit together tbl the st rem on the ndl and the next st. Rep from * to last 5 sts (the first st will be the leftover from the last k2tog tbl); end with p1, k1, p1, sl 2 wyif
Row 3: k3, p1, k1, p2tog slipping only the first loop off the non-working ndl. *Purl tog the st on the ndl and the next st. Rep from * to the last 5 sts (the first st will be the leftover from the last p2tog)); end with k1, p1, k1, sl 2 wyif
Row 4: k3, p1, k1, k2tog tbl slipping only the first loop off the non-working ndl. * Knit tog tbl the st on the ndl and the next st. Rep from * to last 5 sts (the first st will be the leftover from the last k2tog tbl); end with k1, p1, k1, sl 2 wyif

Directions
Work scarf as described in the main pattern, replacing the slip stitch pattern with the Herringbone Stitch. Work Herringbone Stitch with larger ndl and the borders with smaller ndl. Add fringe if desired.

Macramé fringe
Cut 44 lengths of yarn about 30" long. Use a 8" x 15" cardboard template, wrapping yarn for the required number and cutting across one long edge. Attach one length of yarn with an overhand stitch in each stitch across the scarf. At about ¾" from edge, create an overhand knot using the first 4 strands. Rep with the next 4 strands and with each 4-strand group across. About ¾" from the last row of knots, create an overhand knot with first 2 strands, *create an overhand knot using next 4 strands. Rep from * with next 4 strands and with each 4-strand group across. End by knotting remaining 2 strands. Rep row 1 of knotting. Lay scarf on a flat surface and trim fringe evenly.

Variation: Cluster Stitch Scarf
Materials
2 skeins #9408 (Cordovan)

Cluster Stitch
Row 1 (WS): k2, [p1, k1] twice, *p2, yo, rep from * to last 6 sts; end [k1, p1] twice, sl 2 wyif (61 sts)
Row 2: k2, [p1, k1] twice, k3, p3so, *k3, p3so, rep from * to last 6 sts,; end [k1, p1] twice, sl 2 wyif (44 st)
Row 3: k3, p1, k1, p1, *p2, yo, rep from * to last 6 sts; end [p1, k1] twice, sl 2 wyif (61 st)
Row 4: k3, p1, k1, p1, k3, p3so, *k3, p3so, rep from * to last 6 sts; end [p1, k1] twice, sl 2 wyif (44 st)

Directions
CO 45 sts and work Double Seed Stitch Border. On the last row, k2tog before slipping the last 2 sts. Continue as described in the main pattern, replacing the slip stitch pattern with Cluster Stitch. On the first row of the second border, m1 before slipping the last 2 sts. As this stitch pattern has a tendency to bias, wet-blocking is recommended.

Dolman Sleeve Shrug

design by Urban Tribal Wear Designs

Finished sizes
32 (36, 40, 44)"

Gauge
5.5 sts x 7 rows = 1" worked in st st with larger ndl

Materials
5 skeins #9428 (Thyme)
US 7 (4.5 mm) 24" (or longer) circ ndl
US 6 (4.0 mm) 24" circ ndl

Directions
CO 88 (100, 112, 124) sts. Work even in st st for 1½" ending with a WS row. Begin increasing for sleeves as follows: CO 5 sts at the beg of next 2 rows, CO 4 sts at the beg of next 24 rows, then CO 3 sts at beg of next 2 rows (200, 212, 224, 236 total sts). Work even until even sleeve cuff edge measures 4¼" and piece measures about 10" from cast-on edge.

Pattern 216

Front
Work 56 sleeve sts and 24(30, 31, 37) shoulder sts. Join new yarn and bind off 40 (40, 50, 50) center neck sts. Work across rem 24 (30, 31, 37) shoulder sts and 56 sleeve sts. Work 1 WS row. Place front right sts on holder. To shape left front neck, CO 5 sts at the neck edge every other row 3 (3, 4, 4) times, then increase 1 st at neck edge every RS row 5 times. Continue even until the sleeve cuff measures 8½".

Begin sleeve shaping and left front bottom shaping as follows: bind off 3 sts at sleeve edge of next RS row, bind off 4 sts at sleeve edge of next 8 RS rows, then bind off 4 sts at sleeve edge and dec 1 st at center edge on next 4 RS rows. On the following RS row, bind off 5 sts at sleeve edge and dec 1 st at center edge. Bind off remaining 29 (45, 51, 57) left side sts.

Rep for right front, reversing shaping.

Cuffs
With smaller ndl and RS facing, pick up 54 sts along cuff edge. Work in k2, p2 rib for 4". Bind off loosely in rib. Repeat for second cuff.

Finishing
Stitch side seam and underarm seams.

With smaller ndl and RS facing, start at the bottom seam and pick up sts in multiples of 4 all the way around the bottom back, front edge, back neck, and other front edge. Join and pm for beginning of rnd. Work in k2, p2 rib for 4". Bind off loosely in rib.

Variation: Add contrasting trim
Materials
4 skeins #2427 (Glamour; MC)
1 skein #2425 (Provence; CC)

Directions
Work shrug as described in the main pattern. With CC and smaller ndl, work sleeve cuffs to desired length (work for 8" for a fold-back cuff), neck, and body trim.

Variation: Textured Shrug
Materials
4 skeins #9452 (Summer Sky Heather; MC)
1 skein #2433 (Pacific; CC)

Directions
Work shrug as described in the main pattern, following Chart A for the pattern stitch. Establish the pattern with Stitch 2 of the chart.

Variation: Moss Stitch Shrug
Materials
5 skeins #2438 (Spring Meadow)

Directions
Work body and sleeves as described in the main pattern, substituting Moss Stitch for st st. Work trim as described in the main pattern.

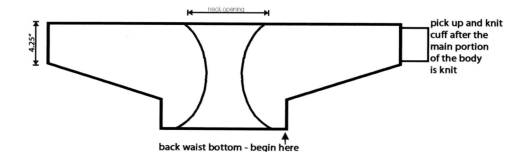

Variation: Long-sleeved Shrug
Materials
5 skeins #2437 (Kansas)

Directions
CO 88 (100, 112, 124) sts. Work even in st st for 1½" ending with a WS row. Begin increasing for sleeves as follows: CO 10 sts at the beg of next 2 rows, CO 6 sts at the beg of next 24 rows, then CO 7 sts at beg of next 2 rows (266, 278, 290, 302 total sts). Work even until even sleeve cuff edge measures 4¼" and piece measures about 10" from cast-on edge.

Front
Work 89 sleeve sts and 24(30, 31, 37) shoulder sts. Join new yarn and bind off 40 (40, 50, 50) center neck sts. Work across rem 24 (30, 31, 37) shoulder sts and 89 sleeve sts. Work 1 WS row. Place front right sts on holder. To shape left front neck, CO 5 sts at the neck edge every other row 3 (3, 4, 4) times, then increase 1 st at neck edge every RS row 5 times. Continue even until the sleeve cuff measures 8½".

Begin sleeve shaping and left front bottom shaping as follows: bind off 7 sts at sleeve edge of next RS row, bind off 6 sts at sleeve edge of next 8 RS rows, then bind off 6 sts at sleeve edge and dec 1 st at center edge on next 4 RS rows. On the following RS row, bind off 10 sts at sleeve edge and dec 1 st at center edge. Bind off remaining 29 (45, 51, 57) left side sts.

Repeat for right front, reversing shaping.

Work cuffs and finish as described in the main pattern.

Moss Stitch

□ knit on right side, purl on wrong side
▨ purl on right side, knit on wrong side

Chart A

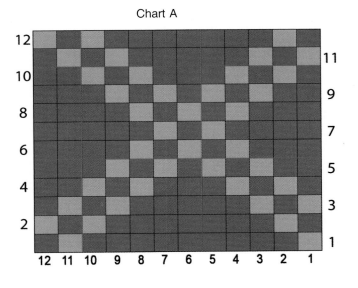

■ purl on right side, knit on wrong side
▨ knit on right side, purl on wrong side

Projects

Abbreviations

approx	approximately
beg	beginning
CC	contrast color
C1, C2, etc.	color 1, color 2, etc.
circ ndl	circular needle
cm	centimeter
cn	cable needle
CO	cast on
cont	continue
dd	double decrease: slip next 2 sts knitwise <u>together</u> onto right needle, k third st, pass 2 sl sts over knit st
dec	decrease
dpn(s)	double-pointed needle(s)
inc	increase
k	knit
k2tog	knit two stitches together (right-slanted decrease)
L	size large
LHN	left-hand needle
LT	left twist. Knit second st tbl and leave on ndl.
M	medium
MC	main color
m1	make one
mm	millimeter
p	purl
p2tog	purl 2 sts together
p3so	pass the 3rd stitch on the right ndl over the 1st two sts and off the ndl.
pm	place marker
ndl	needle
rem	remaining
rep	repeat
rev st st	reverse stockinette stitch
rvs sc	reverse single crochet
RHN	right-hand needle
rnd	round
RS	right side of work
RT	right twist: knit second st through front loop and leave on ndl. Knit first st as usual, then allow both sts to slip off ndl.
S	size small
Sc	single crochet
sl	slip st (purlwise unless otherwise indicated)
ssk	slip 2 sts knitwise, one at a time, then knit together (left-slanted decrease)
st st	stockinette stitch (RS knit, WS purl; or knit each round)
st(s)	stitch(es)
tbl	through back loop
tfl	through front loop
wrap	on a knit row, bring the yarn forward, sl next st as if to purl, move to yarn to back, sl st back to lhn, turn work. on a purl row, yarn to back, sl next st as if to purl, move yarn forward, return st to lhn, turn work.
WS	wrong side of work
wyib	with yarn in back
wyif	with yarn in front
XS	size extra small
XL	size extra large
yo	yarn over

Additional Instructions

Knit Cast On
1. Create a slip knot and place it on the knitting needle.
2. Take the working needle and slip it into the stitch as you would usually to make a knit stitch.
3. Yarnover and create a knit stitch, then slip the new stitch back to the nonworking needle. One stitch created.
4. Repeat steps 2 and 3.

Cable Cast On
1. Create a slip knot and place it on the knitting needle.
2. Take the working needle and slip it into the stitch as you would usually to make a knit stitch.
3. Yarnover and create a knit stitch, then slip the new stitch back to the nonworking needle. One stitch created.
4. Slip the tip of the working needle between the two stitches. Yarnover and create a knit stitch.
5. Slip the new stitch back to the nonworking needle.
6. Repeat steps 4 and 5.

Long-Tailed Cast-On
1. Create a slip knot and place in on a needle tip.
2. Insert the left thumb and index finger between the two strands of yarn. The long tail should be over the thumb and the yarn coming from the ball over the index finger. Spread the thumb and index finger apart. Secure the two pieces of yarn with the remaining fingers of the left hand.
Note: Yarns are shown in different colors to assist in visualizing the flow of the needle for the process of casting on.
3. Bring needle tip UNDER yarn wrapped around the thumb.
4. Lift this yarn up, over, then under the yarn on the index finger.
5. Pull the yarn through the loop around the thumb.
6. Release loop from thumb to create a new stitch on the needle tip. At the same time, re-insert your thumb under the yarn so you can do the next stitch.

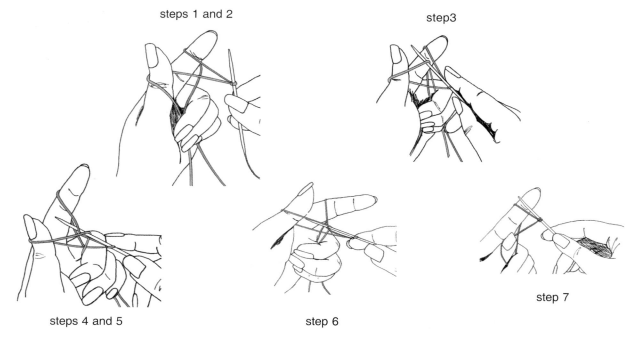

steps 1 and 2

step3

steps 4 and 5

step 6

step 7

92

Provisional Cast On (Long Tail Method)

1. Cut a 24" (or longer depending on the number of stitches required) piece of waste yarn the same weight as your project yarn. Hold the scrap yarn and project yarn together, ends matching, and loosely tie an overhand knot about 8" from the end. The knot will be removed later and should only be tight enough to hold the two pieces of yarn together.

2. Place the needle to which the stitches will cast on between the strands of yarn and against the knot. Cast on the required stitches with the project yarn over your forefinger and the waste yarn over your thumb using the long tail method.
3. Work the project as instructed.
4. Removing the waste yarn - Hold your project with the cast on edge up and the overhand knot at the left.
5. Use the tip of the spare needle to pick up the stitches. Stitches should be picked up from front to back beginning with the first loop. This step is often easier with a needle one size smaller than is called for in the project.

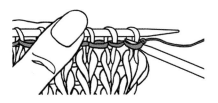

6. After mounting the live stitches insert the point of another needle under the scrap yarn, beginning at the end without a knot) and pull the scrap yarn from the stitch. Continue across, until all the waste yarn has been removed. When the tail of the scrap yarn starts to get long, snip it and continue to remove until all stitches are free. End by untying the knot that holds the waste yarn and project yarn together. Remove the remaining waste yarn. Project yarn will be woven in during finishing.

Knit Stitch

1. Place the needle with the cast on stitches in your left hand and an empty needle in your right hand.
2. With the project yarn coming from the back of the stitches, insert the tip of the right needle from the bottom to top of the first stitch on the LH needle.
3. Bring the yarn from the back of the RH needle, around the left side of the RH needle, and then between the two needles to create a yarnover.

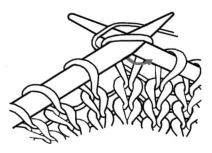

4. Use your right hand to move the needle and loop of yarn toward you and through the stitch, slipping the old stitch off of the LH needle at the same time.
5. Snug the new stitch on the RH needle. One stitch created.

Purl Stitch

1. Place the needle with the cast on stitches in your left and an empty needle in your right hand.
2. Bring the project yarn to the front of the needles and insert the tip of the right needle from the top to bottom of the first stitch on the LH needle.

3. Bring the yarn over the RH needle, then between the two needles to create a yarnover.
4. Use your right hand to move the needle and loop of yarn away you and through the stitch, slipping the old stitch off of the LH needle at the same time.
5. Snug the new stitch on the RH needle. One stitch created.

Knit 1 Below (k1 below)

1. Insert the tip of the needle in to the stitch below the next stitch on the needle
2. Complete a knit stitch and allow the stitch above to slip off the needle when completing.

reverse single crochet (rvs sc)

1. working from left to right, insert the crochet hook into the next stitch to the right.
2. yarn over and pull up a loop.
3. yarn over and draw through both loops on the crochet hook, as you would normally finish an sc.

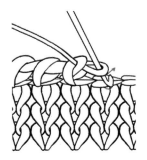

Applied i-cord

1. With RS facing you, CO 3 sts to RHN.
2. With the tip of the RHN, pick up a st in the side of the first row of the garment. (Tail will move to the 3rd st from the needle tip).
3. Take the needle in your left hand and slide stitches toward the tip.
4. K2, slip 1, k1 tbl, psso.
   *With the tip of the RHN, pick a st in the side of the next row of the garment then slide all 4 sts to opposite end of needle. K2, slip 1, k1 tbl, psso. Repeat from * to end of row/round.

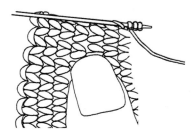

3-st i-cord Bind Off

1. With RS facing you, CO 3 sts to RHN (similar to above), then slip st to LH needle (tail will move to the 3rd st from the needle tip).
2. k2, skp
3. Slip the 3 stitches from RH needle back to the LH needle.
4. steps 2 and 3 until all the sts are bound off. Cut yarn and thread on tapestry needle, pull end of yarn through remaining 3 sts and fasten off.

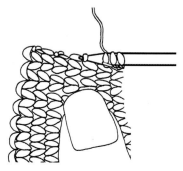

3-Needle Bind Off and Knitted Hem

Used to join to knitted pieces, such as in a shoulder seam or a folded hem
1. The stitches to be joined should be on 2 separate needles.
2. Hold the needles together in one hand. The pattern will dictate whether right or wrong sides of fabric should be facing each other.
3. Insert a third needle into the first stitch on the front needle then the first stitch on the 2nd needle.
4. Knit both stitches together as one.
5. To bind off using this method, repeat steps 3 and 4 then slip the 2nd stitch on

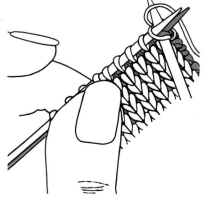

the working needle over the first and off the needle (as in a traditional bind off).
6. Repeat step 5 until one stitch remains on the third needle. Clip yarn and pull tail through last stitch. Finish as directed in pattern.
7. For a knitted hem, repeat steps 3 and 4 until all stitches on both needles have been worked and a single set of stitches are on the working needle.

Whipstitch

1. Thread blunt tip tapestry ndl with yarn.
2. Fold hem where indicated (usually purl a ridge or picot edge).
3. Pick up one st from cast on edge and one corresponding st from side of garment and pull yarn through. Be careful not to pull too tightly.
4. Repeat step 3 to end of row. Clip yarn and weave in end.

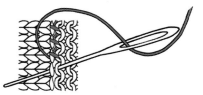

Incr-R (a lifted increase)

1. With the tip of the working needle, lift the right leg of the stitch below the next stitch to be worked.
2. Place the stitch in front of the first st on the nonworking needle, then knit or purl as directed.
3. Work the next stitch as usual

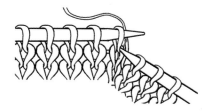

Incr-L (a lifted increase)

1. With the tip of the working needle, lift the left leg of the stitch in the row below the first stitch on the working needle.
2. Place the stitch in front of the first st on the nonworking needle, then knit or purl as directed.
3. Work the next stitch as usual

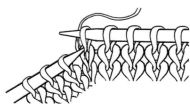

notes

notes